# Bible Nurture and Reader Series

From a child thou hast known
The HOLY SCRIPTURES
which are able to make
thee wise unto salvation.

# Bible Nurture and Reader Series

## Stories About God's People

## Grade 2

### Units 1, 2, 3

**Rod and Staff Publishers, Inc.**

Crockett, Kentucky 41413

# Bible Nurture and Reader Series

This book is designed as part of a series and will be most useful if so used. The series is planned to provide reading textbooks and workbooks for all the pupil will need in reading, phonics, language, spelling, and writing in Grade Two. The series for Grade Two provides 150 lessons. Each lesson has three divisions: *Reader, Reading Workbook,* and *Language Skills Workbook.* All the lessons are based on Bible stories.

In recent years phonics is being recognized as a superior approach to learning to read. Many teachers and school boards are discovering that the child gains reading independence much earlier by phonics than by other methods they have used. In Grade One of this series, the child was taught the sounds of letters and combinations of letters and Grade Two of this series thoroughly reviews what was learned in Grade One and gives further practice, not only in learning to sound and read more new words, but also in spelling them.

There is one teacher's manual and there are ten pupil's texts and workbooks arranged as follows:

## Grade Two Curriculum

Teacher's Manual

Pupil's Reader   Units 1, 2, 3
Pupil's Reader   Units 4, 5

Language Skills Workbook  Unit 1
Language Skills Workbook  Units 2, 3
Language Skills Workbook  Units 4, 5

Reading Workbook Unit 1
Reading Workbook Unit 2
Reading Workbook Unit 3
Reading Workbook Unit 4
Reading Workbook Unit 5

Revised, 1970
Copyright, 1964
By
Rod and Staff Publishers, Inc.
Crockett, Kentucky 41413
Printed in U. S. A.


Code no. 70-7-86

# Table of Contents

# Unit 1

We Review Genesis and Job

# Unit ❷

## Moses Leads
## God's People

# Unit **3**

## More About Moses
## Balaam
## Israel in Canaan

# Unit **1**

## We Review Genesis
## and Job

# Bible Memory Verses

1. In every thing give thanks.  1 Thessalonians 5:18

2. The Lord is my helper.  Hebrews 13:6

3. Let him that stole steal no more.  Ephesians 4:28

4. Lie not one to another.  Colossians 3:9

5. They that seek the Lord understand all things. Proverbs 28:5

6. Forgive, and ye shall be forgiven.  Luke 6:37

# God Made the Earth

Genesis 1 and 2

There was a time when there was no
earth. So, of course, there were no
plants, animals, fish, birds, or people.
There was no sun, moon, or stars.
Then God made all these things in just
six days. First He made the heaven
and the earth. Then He made light and
divided the light from the darkness.
He called the light day and the darkness
He called night. On the second day He
made the sky where the birds fly. He
divided the land and the water on the
third day. He also made the green
things to grow on the earth. On the
fourth day He made the sun, moon,
and stars to shine on the earth and
give light. The sun was made to give

us light in the daytime, and the moon
and the stars were made to give us
light at night. The next day was the
fifth day. On this day God made the
fish and the birds. On the sixth day
God made the animals and man. The
first man was Adam. God gave him
that name.

On the seventh day God rested from
all His work. No one but God could do
such great work, and God had done it
in just six days. God worked six days
and rested one day, and that is what
He wants His people to do.

God used the dust of the earth to
make Adam. Then He breathed into
his nose and Adam was alive. To make
a wife for Adam, God put Adam to
sleep and took out one of his ribs.
From this rib He made a woman. So
when Adam woke up from his deep
sleep, he found he had a wife. God
put them into a very nice garden to

live. It was called the Garden of Eden. A river ran through and watered the garden. Every kind of tree grew in this garden. From these trees they could get good food to eat. God told them that they could eat from every tree in the garden except one. There was one tree from which He did not want them to eat. That tree was in the middle of the garden. God told them that they would die if they would eat from that tree.

God brought the animals to Adam to see what he would name them. Whatever name Adam gave to an animal, that was its name. He also named his wife. He called her Eve. At this time they were the only two people on the earth. There were no children.

# The First Sin

Genesis 3

Adam and Eve were very happy in their new home. There was no sin there. But one day a snake came to Eve and talked to her. He said, "Has God said that you should not eat of every tree in the garden?"

Eve answered, "We may eat of the trees in the garden. But of the tree that is in the middle of the garden, God said that we should not eat of it or we will die."

The serpent said, "You shall not die, for God knows that when you eat of it, you will be as gods."

Of course, what the serpent said was not true because God said they would die, and God never tells a lie.

Eve should not have listened to the serpent. But she looked at the tree and saw that the fruit on it looked good to eat. So she took some and ate it. She gave some to Adam and he also ate it.

They knew then how bad it feels to sin. They both were very much afraid. They tried to hide so that God could not see them. But they could not hide from God. God knew what they had done, and He had to punish them.

First He punished the serpent. He told him that he would have to go on his belly and eat dust all his life. He told Eve that she would have a lot of sorrow. God said to Adam, "Because you listened to Eve, and have eaten of the tree of which I told you not to eat, the ground will have thistles and thorns You will have to work hard to get food to eat. You will sweat until you go back to the ground. You were taken out of the ground, for you are dust, and you will go back to dust."

Then God sent them out of the garden. They could no longer eat from the fruit there.

But God still loved them. He made them coats of skin. Best of all, He promised to send Jesus who would die to save them from their sins.

Lesson 3

# Cain and Abel

Genesis 4:1-15

After Adam and Eve sinned and were driven from the Garden of Eden, God gave them a baby boy. This was the first baby because Adam and Eve had never been babies. They named this first baby Cain. After a while God gave them another baby boy. His name was Abel.

These boys grew to be men. Cain worked in the ground and raised food but Abel's work was to take care of sheep. After a time Cain and Abel each brought an offering to God. Cain brought food that he had raised, and Abel brought one of his sheep.

God was pleased with Abel and the offering that he brought. But God was not pleased with Cain and his offering.

Cain became angry because God did not like what he had brought. Then God spoke to Cain and said, "Why are you angry? If you do what is right, will I not be pleased? But if you do not do what is right, there is sin."

But Cain did not ask God to take away his sin. Instead, he sinned more. One day Cain talked with Abel when they were together in the field, and Cain killed Abel.

The Lord said to Cain, "Where is your brother Abel?"

Cain answered, "I do not know. Am I supposed to take care of my brother?"

But God said, "What have you done? Your brother's blood cries to Me from the ground."

Then God punished Cain for the terrible thing that he had done. He told Cain that from now on when he planted things, they would not grow well for him. He would wander around like a tramp.

Cain said to God, "This punishment is more than I can stand." He was afraid someone would kill him. God put a mark on Cain so that no one would kill him.

## Lesson 4
# The Big Flood
Genesis 6:5-8:5

After a time there were many
people on the earth. But the sad
thing was that most of these people
lived wicked lives. They did not
love God.

God felt sorry that He had made
man on the earth. He said, "I will
destroy the people that I have made,
and the animals and birds, too,
because I am sorry that I made
them."

There was one man on the earth
who loved God and tried to please
Him. His name was Noah. He had
a wife and three sons. He was not
like most of the people. The Lord
did not want to destroy this man. So

God said to him, "Make an ark of wood and put pitch on the outside and on the inside. Make a window in the ark and put a door in the side of it." God also told him just how to make it and how big it should be.

God told Noah that He was going to send a flood on the earth to destroy the people and animals. He told Noah to take with him into the ark seven of each kind of some of the animals and two of each of the other kinds of animals. He was also to take some of each kind of food to keep them alive while the flood was on the earth.

Noah did everything just as God told him to do. Seven days before God sent the rain, He told Noah and his family to go into the ark. They took some of every creeping thing, animal, beast, and bird. They all went into the ark, and God shut the door.

Then all the fountains of the great

deep were broken up and it began to rain. It rained forty days and forty nights. Each day the water came up higher and higher. Every mountain on the whole earth was covered and the bad people were destroyed. But Noah and his family were safe in the ark on top of the water. The water could not hurt them. They had obeyed God and God took care of them.

After a time the water began to go down again. Each day the water went down until one day the ark was resting on the top of a mountain. Soon they could see the tops of other mountains above the waters, but still it was not time for them to go out of the ark.

## Lesson 5

# After the Flood

Genesis 8:6-9:17 and 11:1-9

One day Noah opened the window of the ark and sent out a big black bird called a raven. It flew around over the water until the water was gone down. Noah also sent out a dove but she could not find a place to land because of the water. So she came back to the ark. Noah put out his hand and took her back into the ark. He waited seven days and then he let the dove out again. The dove came back to him in the evening. This time she had a leaf in her mouth. By this Noah could tell the waters were going down. In seven more days he sent the dove out again. But this time the dove did not come back to the ark.

Noah and his family were in the ark a long time. They were there over a year. By then the ground was dry, and God said that they should go out of the ark. So Noah and his wife went out. His three sons and their wives and all the animals went out of the ark.

Noah was thankful for what God had done for him. God had kept him safe. He made an offering to God. God was pleased with this offering. He promised that He would never again destroy the earth with a flood. He put a rainbow in the sky to show the promise He had made.

After a time there were many people on the earth again. Many of them did not love God. Everyone spoke the same language. Some of these people got together and decided to build a tower. They wanted it to be a very high tower.

They did not have a good reason
for building this tower, and God was
not pleased with what they were doing.
He changed their way of speaking.
When they tried to talk to each other,
they could not understand what was
being said. Then they could not finish
building the tower. Instead, they went
away from each other to live in
different parts of the earth.

# Abram and Lot

Genesis 11:27-13:15

Abram lived in a land called Ur. He moved with his father to a different place. Abram's wife, Sarah, and his brother's son, Lot, went along with him.

God had said to Abram, "Get out of this country. Go away from your father and come to a land that I will show you."

Abram started out with his wife, Sarah, and Lot, his brother's son. They took with them all their things and their servants. When they got to the land of Canaan, God told Abram that He would give him that land. Abram did not build a house and stay in one place. He lived in a tent and

moved from place to place. Wherever
he went, he built an altar and
worshiped God.

There came a time when the crops
did not grow well in this land. So they
went down into a strange land. But
after they were there for some time
the king of that land sent them away.
They went back to the land of Canaan.

The Lord was with Abram and by
this time he was a very rich man. He
had many animals but Lot also had
many animals and that made trouble.
There was not enough room for
Abram's cattle and Lot's cattle to
live so near each other. The men
who took care of the cattle began to
quarrel.

Abram did not want to quarrel. He
said to Lot, "Let us not quarrel. You
go away from me. If you go to the
left, I will go to the right. If you go
to the right, I will go to the left." It

was kind of Abram to let Lot choose first. He was not selfish but Lot was selfish. Lot chose the land that looked the best. But this land was near two cities and the people in these cities were very wicked. It was not good for Lot and his family to live in the city of Sodom with such wicked people near them. It did not pay Lot to be selfish.

After Lot was gone, God told Abram to look north and south and east and west. Then God said, "All the land that you see I will give to you and to your children."

# Abraham Prays

Genesis 17:1-19 and 18:16-19:26

Abram and Sarah became old.
When Abram was nearly one hundred
years old, God changed his name to
Abraham. God promised Abraham that
he and Sarah would have a son. They
could hardly believe the good news.
God even told them what to name the
baby. He said that his name should be
Isaac.

You remember that the people in
the city where Lot lived were wicked.
They were so wicked that God was
going to destroy them. Because
Abraham was God's friend, God told
Abraham what he was going to do. He
told him that He was going to destroy
the city. Of course, Abraham thought

about Lot. Lot was in that city! Did that mean Lot would be destroyed, too? Abraham did not want Lot to be destroyed. So Abraham said, "Will You destroy the good people with the wicked people? If there are fifty good people in the city, will you destroy it?"

God said, "If I find fifty good people in the city, I will not destroy it."

Abraham was afraid there might not be fifty good people in the city. So he said, "Will You destroy it if there are five less than fifty?"

"No," God said. "If I find forty-five good people in the city, I will not destroy it."

But Abraham thought there might not be that many good people. Finally he asked God whether He would destroy the city if there were only ten good people there. God promised that He would not. Then the Lord went away and Abraham went home.

The Lord did not find even ten good people in that big city. But because Abraham did not want Lot to be destroyed, God sent two angels to Lot to warn him to get out of the city. They said, "Get out of the city. God is going to destroy it."

Lot told his sons-in-law that God was going to destroy the city, but they did not believe it. They did not want to leave the city, and Lot did not want to go and leave them behind.

Finally the angels had to take hold of the hands of Lot and his wife and his two daughters who were not married and bring them out of the city. God told them not to look back. Lot's wife did not obey. She looked back and was turned into salt.

After Lot was out of the city, God sent fire down from heaven and burned the city and the people in it.

# A Test for Abraham

Genesis 21:1-8 and 22:1-19

God promised Abraham and Sarah that He would give them a baby. So, that is just what God did. We can always be sure that God will keep His promises.

Little Baby Isaac was born when Abraham was one hundred years old. This was Sarah's only child. They were very happy and they loved him very much.

Of course, little Isaac grew. God knew that Abraham and Sarah loved Isaac. So He gave Abraham a very hard test. The test was to prove Abraham's love for God. Did he love God more than Isaac, or did he love Isaac more than he loved God?

God said to Abraham, "Take your son, your only son Isaac, and offer him to Me." That meant he should kill his son. If Abraham loved God the most, he would obey God and give up Isaac or anything else God would ask of him. But if he loved Isaac more than God, he would not obey God and he would keep Isaac.

God told Abraham where he was to go to offer Isaac to the Lord. Because Abraham loved God the most, he was ready to do what God said. He got up early in the morning and took along Isaac and two other men. The mountain where he was to take Isaac was a long way from home, and it took three days for them to get there.

The two men who went along with Abraham and Isaac did not go along up on the mountain. Abraham and Isaac went together.

When they came to the place where

God had told them to go, Abraham
made an altar. He bound Isaac and
put him on the wood on the altar.
Then he took the knife to kill his son.

But just then he heard something.
Someone said, "Abraham! Abraham!"
It was God's angel calling to him from
heaven.

Abraham answered, "Here I am."
The angel said, "Do not do anything
to your son." He also said that now
he knew that Abraham loved and
feared God because he had obeyed
Him.

How happy Abraham must have
been! He had been willing to obey
God, and now he could keep his son,
too.

When Abraham looked around, he
saw an animal that was caught in the
brush. He took it and offered it to
God instead of offering Isaac.

Then the angel talked to Abraham

again and told him that because he had obeyed God, God would be with him. God was pleased with Abraham because he had obeyed Him even when He asked him to do a very hard thing.

# A Wife for Isaac

Genesis 23:1-2 and 24:1-67

When Isaac was about thirty-seven years old, his mother Sarah died. After this Abraham wanted to help Isaac get a good wife. Very many people in the land where Abraham now lived were wicked people. They did not love God. Abraham wanted Isaac's wife to be from his own people.

Abraham called his oldest servant to him and told him to go back to his country and find a wife for Isaac. The servant was afraid that he could not find a woman who would be willing to leave home and go with him to a strange land. But Abraham told him that God would help him.

The man took ten camels and went.
When he came to the city where
Abraham had lived, he took the camels
to a well of water. It was just the
time of the day when women came to the
well to get water.

There by the well, Abraham's
servant prayed to God and asked
God to help him know who was the
right woman to be Isaac's wife. If
he would say to a woman, "Give me
a drink," and the woman would say,
"Drink, and I will also give your
camels a drink," then he would know
that it was the right woman.

While the servant was still praying,
a woman came to the well to get
water. She went down to the well and
got some water and came back up
again.

The servant said to the woman,
"Let me drink a little water."

She said, "Drink, and I will get

water for your camels, also."

The servant asked her who she was. She told him that Abraham's brother was her grandfather. The servant was very happy because he knew that God had helped him to find the right woman. He bowed his head and thanked God, but the woman ran home to tell her family all about it.

This young woman's name was Rebekah. When her brother, Laban, heard about the man at the well, he went to find him and invited him to come home with him. The servant went home with Laban, but he would not eat until he had told them why he had come.

After they heard the whole story, they said that Rebekah could go. Rebekah was willing to leave home to be Isaac's wife.

The servant took Rebekah and they went back to Abraham and Isaac. Isaac loved his wife and took her to her new home which had been his mother's tent.

# The Twins

Genesis 25:21-26:33

For a long time Isaac and Rebekah had no children. They wanted children, so Isaac asked the Lord for a child. The Lord was very good to them and gave them more than they asked for. He gave them twin boys! Although many twins look very much alike, these did not. They not only looked different but they were different. Esau grew up to be a good hunter. His father Isaac was glad that Esau could hunt because he liked to eat the meat Esau would bring to him. Jacob worked at home.

One day Esau came in from the field very tired and wanted something to eat. Jacob had made some red soup. Esau asked Jacob to give him some of the red soup.

Now Esau had something that Jacob wanted very much. Esau had a right to have two times as much of his father's things after his father died. Jacob wanted to have this right. It was called a birthright. Jacob thought maybe he could trade with Esau. He told Esau that he would give him the soup if Esau would give him the birthright. Esau was afraid he would die if he did not get something to eat. He sold his birthright to Jacob so that Jacob would give him some soup.

In the land where Isaac and Rebekah and the twins lived, there came a time when they had hardly enough to eat. But God talked to Isaac and told him where to go so that he would have a good crop. Isaac moved to this place and planted a crop. God made it grow, and it gave them a lot of food. There they had plenty to eat, and Isaac became a very rich man.

The people who lived near Isaac saw that Isaac was very rich and that he had more than they. This made them feel jealous and mean. They filled Isaac's wells with dirt so that he could not get water from them.

At last the king told Isaac to go away. So Isaac moved a little farther away. Isaac's servants dug a well. It was a good well but some other men came and said that it was their well. Even though Isaac knew the well was his, he would not quarrel. Instead, he had his servants dig another well. But the men came and took that well away from him, too. Still Isaac would not quarrel. He just let them have it and went away and dug another well.

God was pleased with Isaac and promised to be with him.

## Lesson 11
# How Jacob Got the Blessing
Genesis 27:1-29

By and by Isaac became an old man. In his old age he was blind.

One day he called Esau to him and said, "I am old. I do not know when I will die. Please go out into the field and get me some meat. Fix it the way I like it and bring it to me so that I can eat it and bless you before I die." To bless someone means to ask God to give him good things.

Esau did as his father said and went out to kill a deer so that he could fix the meat for his father to eat.

Rebekah heard what Isaac had said to Esau. She wanted Jacob to get the blessing instead of Esau. So she

thought of a plan to get Isaac to bless Jacob instead of Esau.

She said to Jacob, "I heard your father tell Esau to bring him some meat so that he can bless him before he dies. Now, my son, do just as I tell you. Go and get two good kids. I will make the meat the way your father likes it. Then you take it to your father, and he will eat it and bless you."

Rebekah thought that since Isaac was blind, he would think it was Esau bringing in the meat and he would eat it and bless Jacob, thinking that he was blessing Esau. But Jacob was afraid his father would feel him and find out that he was not Esau. Then maybe his father would ask God to give him bad things instead of blessing him, and he did not want that.

But his mother told him to obey

her. So he did as he was told to do. She put Esau's clothes on Jacob, gave him the meat, and sent him to his father.

Jacob came to his father and said, "My father."

His father answered, "Here I am. Who are you?"

Jacob said, "I am Esau. I did what you told me to do. Please get up and eat my meat so that you can bless me."

Isaac asked, "How did you find it so quickly, my son?"

"Because the Lord brought it to me," said Jacob.

"Come near, so that I can feel whether you are really my son Esau," said Isaac.

After Isaac felt Jacob he was really puzzled. He felt like Esau because of the way his mother had fixed him up, but when he talked, he sounded like

Jacob.

"Are you really Esau?" asked
Isaac.

Jacob answered, "I am."

Isaac ate the meat and gave Jacob
the blessing, but he thought he was
giving it to Esau.

## Lesson 12
# Jacob Leaves Home
Genesis 27:30-28:22

Jacob had just left the room where his father was when Esau came in. He also had meat fixed the way his father liked it. He said to his father, "Let my father get up and eat of his son's meat so that you can bless me."

"Who are you?" asked Isaac.

"I am your son Esau," he answered.

Poor old Isaac trembled very much. He said, "I ate before you came and blessed him. Yes, and he will be blessed."

Esau cried very hard when he heard this. He said, "Bless me, even me also, O my father!"

But Isaac said, "Your brother came and took away your blessing."

Esau said, "He took away my
birthright, and now he has taken
away my blessing. Don't you have
a blessing left for me?"

Isaac had already given the blessing
to Jacob, and it was too late for Esau
to have it. But he gave Esau a very
small blessing.

Now Esau hated his twin brother
for what he had done. He hated him
so much that he decided to kill him
after his father was dead.

Rebekah found out that Esau wanted
to kill Jacob. So she called Jacob and
said, "Your brother Esau plans to
kill you. Now obey me and go to my
brother Laban. Stay there until your
brother is not angry anymore. Then
I will send and get you from there."

Isaac also wanted Jacob to go to
Laban and get a wife there. He wanted
him to get one of Laban's daughters to
be his wife. Do you remember that

Laban was Rebekah's brother? So
Laban was Jacob's uncle.

Jacob left home and started out for
his Uncle Laban's home. He could not
get there in one day. After the sun
went down, he stopped. He got some
stones for pillows and lay down to
sleep. There, as he lay asleep, he
dreamed a strange dream. He dreamed
that he saw a ladder that reached from
earth to heaven. God's angels were
going up and down on this ladder. The
Lord stood above the ladder and talked
to Jacob. He said, "I am the Lord
God of Abraham your father, and the
God of Isaac. The land you are on I
will give to you and your children.
I am with you and will keep you
wherever you go and will bring you
back to this land."

When Jacob woke up, he was afraid.
He said, "The Lord is in this place
and I did not know it." Then Jacob

promised the Lord that he would let Him be his God if He would do all these things for him.

# Jacob Works for Laban

Genesis 29:1-30

Jacob got up early in the morning and went on his way again. He finally reached the land where his Uncle Laban lived. In the field he saw a well to which people came to get water for their sheep. At the mouth of the well was a large stone which had to be rolled back before they could draw water for their sheep. Some men came and rolled back the stone. They gave water to the sheep and then put the stone back in place again.

Jacob asked these men whether they knew Laban. They said they knew him and that his daughter Rachel was coming with her father's sheep because she took care of them.

When Jacob saw her coming, he went to the well, rolled back the stone, and gave water to Laban's sheep. He told Rachel who he was, and Rachel ran and told her father.

When Laban heard that his sister's son had come, he ran to meet him, kissed him, and brought him to his house.

After Jacob had been with his Uncle Laban for a month, Laban said to Jacob, "Should you work for me for nothing? Tell me what your wages should be."

Now Laban had two daughters. Rachel had an older sister whose name was Leah. Jacob wanted the younger one, Rachel, to be his wife. So he said to Laban, "I will work for you seven years for Rachel."

Laban did not know of any other man he would rather have Rachel marry. So he told Jacob to stay with him.

Jacob worked seven years so that he could have Rachel for his wife. The time did not seem long to Jacob because he loved Rachel very much.

After the seven years were finished, Jacob asked Laban to give him his wife. But Laban played a mean trick on Jacob and gave him Leah instead of Rachel.

Jacob said, "What is this that you have done to me? Did I not work for Rachel?"

But Laban said, "In our land we must not give the younger one before the older one. If you work for me seven more years, you can have Rachel, too."

Laban gave Rachel to Jacob, too. He worked seven more years for her. He loved Rachel more than Leah.

# Jacob Leaves Laban

Genesis 30:25-31:55

Jacob had a big family of eleven sons and one daughter. Now Jacob decided it was time to leave Laban and go back to the land where his father lived.

Jacob asked Laban to let him go, but Laban did not want to let him go. God had made things go better for him when Jacob was there. So Jacob stayed and worked for him. God made things go well for Jacob so that he became a very rich man.

One day God said to Jacob, "Go back to the land of your fathers and I will be with you." So Jacob got ready to go. He put his wives and children on camels. He took his animals and everything he had. Rachel stole her father's idols, but Jacob did not know it. They left without even telling Laban that they were going. He was away from home at the time, and he did not find out for three days that they had gone.

When Laban found out that Jacob had left without telling him, he did not like it. But he could not really blame Jacob for leaving. He had not been very nice to Jacob when he was there. God had told Jacob to leave.

Laban took some men and went after Jacob, but it took them seven days to catch up with him.

Laban asked Jacob why he had gone without telling him.

Jacob said, "Because I was afraid you would take your daughters from me."

Laban was not pleased that his idols had been stolen, but of course Jacob did not know that Rachel had taken them. So Jacob told Laban that he could look for anything that belonged to him and take it. He also said that whoever had his idols should not live.

So Laban went to look for his idols. He looked in all the tents. Last of all he came to Rachel's tent. He looked and looked. They were in the tent but he did not find them because Rachel was sitting on them.

Jacob was angry with Laban for coming after him as he had. Jacob had worked hard for Laban, and Laban had not given him good wages for all his hard work. Jacob was a rich man only because God had been so good to him.

But they promised they would never hurt each other. Early the next morning, Laban got up and kissed them good-bye and went back home.

# Jacob Is Afraid

Genesis 32:1-33:15 and 35:1-29

Jacob was on his way home once more, but there was one thing he wondered about. He had left home because Esau, his twin brother, hated him and wanted to kill him. Would it be safe for him to go home? He sent men on ahead to talk to Esau and told them just what to say.

The men came back with news that made Jacob very much afraid. They said, "We came to your brother Esau and he is coming with four hundred men to meet you." Did that mean Esau wanted to kill them? Poor Jacob did not know. He prayed to God and asked God to help him so that Esau would not kill them.

Jacob got a big present ready for some of his men to take ahead for Esau. It was about five hundred eighty animals of different kinds. Jacob thought if he would give Esau a big present it would help Esau not to be angry with him.

That night, when Jacob was all alone, a man came and wrestled with him. Jacob did not know who it was, but they wrestled until morning. Finally, the man put Jacob's hip out of joint. He said, "From now on your name will be Israel." Then he blessed him and left. Now Jacob knew that God was the One who had talked to him, and he knew that God would help him.

When Jacob looked up, he saw his brother Esau. He had four hundred men with him. Jacob went to meet him and bowed himself to the ground before him. Esau ran to meet Jacob and kissed him. They seemed very happy to see each other. After they had talked awhile, Esau went home, and Jacob went on to the land of Canaan.

After they were in the land of Canaan for a while, God told Jacob to move to Bethel. Bethel was the name of the place where Jacob had slept on his way to his Uncle Laban's house.

Some of the people at Jacob's house still had idols. Jacob told them to get rid of their idols before they went on to Bethel. So they gave them to Jacob, and he hid them under a tree. Then they went on to Bethel.

After a while they left Bethel. As they were on the way, God gave Rachel another son. Jacob named him Benjamin. Her other son's name was Joseph. Now Joseph had a baby brother, and Jacob had twelve sons!

Benjamin's mother, Rachel, died when he was born. Now the wife that Jacob loved most was gone.

At last Jacob got back home to his father Isaac. He had not seen him for more than twenty years. When Jacob had left home, his father was old and did not expect to live very long, but now he was still alive. But Isaac died after this, and his sons, Jacob and Esau, buried him.

# Joseph's Dreams

Genesis 37:1-11

Jacob had twelve sons. Of all these sons, he loved Joseph the most. He made him a coat of many colors.

It was easy for the other brothers to see that their father loved Joseph more than he loved them. This made them jealous. They hated Joseph so much that they could not even talk nicely to him.

When Joseph helped his brothers to take care of his father's sheep, he saw his brothers do things that were wrong. He told his father what they did.

One time Joseph had a dream. He dreamed that he and his brothers were out in the field, binding sheaves. His sheaf stood up and his brothers'

sheaves stood around his sheaf and
bowed down to it.

When Joseph told this dream to his
brothers, they hated him all the more.
Did this dream mean that someday
Joseph would become a great man
and that they would be his servants
and bow down to him? They did not
want Joseph to be a great man, and
they did not want to bow down to him!

Joseph dreamed another dream, and
again he told it to his brothers. He
said, "I have dreamed another dream.
The sun and the moon and eleven stars
bowed down to me."

His father said, "What is this
dream that you have dreamed? Shall
I and your mother and brothers bow
down to you?"

These dreams made Joseph's
brothers jealous. But Joseph's
father remembered the dreams to
see what would come of them.

Lesson 17

# A Wicked Plan

Genesis 37:12-25

Do you remember that God had changed Jacob's name to Israel? So we call him Israel, too. Israel was Joseph's father.

One day when ten of Joseph's brothers were away from home taking care of their father's sheep, Israel sent Joseph to them. He said, "See whether your brothers and the flocks are getting along all right. Then come back and tell me."

Joseph went but they were not where he expected to find them. As he was walking around in a field, looking for them, a man saw him and asked him, "For what are you looking?"

Joseph answered, "I am looking for my brothers. Please tell me where they are."

The man told Joseph where to look for them. Joseph found them in the place that the man had told him to look.

When Joseph was still quite a long way off, his brothers saw him coming. Wicked thoughts came into their minds. They decided to kill him. They thought that if they would kill him, his dreams could not come true. They could tell their father that some bad animal had eaten him. Of course, they would not want their father to know that they had killed him.

Joseph's oldest brother did not want them to kill him. He said, "Let us not kill him. Let us just put him into a pit."

He did not tell his brothers, but when they did not see him, he planned to take Joseph out of the pit and let him go back to his father. The other brothers thought Joseph would die in the pit.

Poor Joseph was coming nearer and nearer. He did not know what his wicked brothers were planning to do to him. When Joseph came to them, they took off his coat of many colors. They took him and put him into a dry, empty pit. Then the brothers sat down to eat.

## Lesson 18

# Joseph Is Sold

Genesis 37:25-36 and 39:1-6

The brothers looked up and saw a group of men with camels. They were on their way to a strange land called Egypt.

One of the brothers got an idea. He said, "What good will it do us if we kill our brother? Let us sell him to these men." So they took Joseph up out of the pit and sold him to these strange men for twenty pieces of silver.

Poor Joseph felt very sad. He was going away with men whom he did not even know. He was going farther and farther from his home and his father. And his own brothers had done this to him.

Joseph's oldest brother was not
there when the other brothers sold
Joseph. He did not know what they
had done. When he came back to the
pit, Joseph was gone. He went to tell
his brothers about it, but, of course,
they already knew what had happened.
The oldest brother felt bad because he
had planned to let Joseph go back to
his father. Now it was too late.

The brothers took a kid, killed it,
and dipped Joseph's coat into its blood.
They brought it to their father and
said, "We found this. Do you know
whether it is your son's coat or not?"

Israel knew that it was Joseph's
coat. He said, "It is my son's coat.
A bad animal has eaten him. Joseph
is torn in pieces."

For many days poor Israel cried.
He did not know that his sons had not
told him the truth. The children tried
to make him feel better. But Israel

felt very sad. He thought he would
be sad until he died.

But what had happened to Joseph?
He was taken down into the land of
Egypt and sold as a servant to one of
the king's men.

God was with Joseph and helped
him. Joseph's master could see that
God was with him. He liked Joseph
and was very kind to him. He made
Joseph the chief servant. God blessed
Joseph's master while Joseph was
there.

# Joseph in Prison

Genesis 39:7-40:13

Joseph's master was very kind to Joseph, but his master's wife was a wicked woman. She tried to get Joseph to sin. Although she tried day after day, Joseph would not sin. One day she tried very, very hard to get Joseph to sin, but he would not. She did not like it and got Joseph into trouble.

When the master came home, she told him a lie. She said that Joseph had done a very wicked thing. She did not tell him that she had tried to make him do the wicked thing and Joseph would not do it.

The master believed what his wife told him. He was angry with Joseph.

He had him put into prison where the king's prisoners were kept.

God was with Joseph in the prison. He made it so that the keeper of the prison liked Joseph. He let Joseph look after the other prisoners.

One day the king in Egypt became angry with two of his men and had them put into the prison where Joseph was. One of these men had been the king's butler, and the other man had been the king's baker.

One morning when Joseph came in to where they were, he saw that they looked sad. He asked them, "Why do you look so sad today?"

They said, "We dreamed a dream, and no one can tell us what it means."

Joseph told them that God could tell what their dreams meant. He asked them to tell him their dreams.

First the butler told his dream. He said, "In my dream, I saw a

vine. In the vine were three branches
with grapes on them. I took the
grapes, pressed them into the king's
cup, and gave them to the king."

Joseph said, "This is what your
dream means. The three branches
are three days. In three days the
king will let you go back and work
for him. You can give the cup to the
king as you did before."

# The King Dreams

Genesis 40:14-41:9

This was good news for the butler. In just three days he would be able to get out of prison and go back to work for the king. It gave Joseph new hope of getting out of prison. He said to the butler, "When you are back in the king's house, tell the king about me. I was stolen away from home, and I have done nothing bad that I should be put into prison." Joseph thought if the king knew this, he might let him out of prison.

When the baker saw that the butler's dream meant something good, he also told his dream. He said, "I had three white baskets on my head. In the top basket were all kinds of baked things for the king. The birds ate them out of the basket on my head."

Joseph said, "The baskets are three days. In three days the king will hang you on a tree, and the birds will eat you."

Everything happened to the butler and baker just as Joseph said. In three days the king had a birthday. He made a feast for all his servants. He let the butler come back to work for him, but he hanged the baker.

The butler forgot about Joseph. He did not tell the king what Joseph wanted him to say. So Joseph had to stay in prison. Two years went by. Then the king had a dream. He dreamed that he stood by a river. Seven fat cows came up out of the river and ate in the field. Then seven thin cows came up out of the river and ate the seven fat cows. But after they had eaten the fat cows, they were as thin as they had been before they ate the fat cows.

After this dream the king woke up. He went back to sleep and dreamed again. This time he saw seven good ears of corn come up on one stalk. Seven thin ears came up after them. The thin ears ate the good ones.

In the morning the king was troubled. He wanted to know the meaning of these two strange dreams. He called in his wise men and told them the dreams. Not one of them could tell the king what his dreams meant. Then the butler remembered something. What do you think it was?

Lesson 21

# Joseph Helps the King

Genesis 41:9-57

The butler told the king about Joseph. He said, "The baker and I dreamed the same night while we were in prison. Joseph told us what our dreams meant, and everything happened just as Joseph said."

The king sent for Joseph. The men hurried to get Joseph out of the prison and to bring him to the king. Joseph cleaned up, put on other clothes, and came in to the king.

The king said to Joseph, "I have dreamed a dream, and no one can tell me what it means. I have heard that you can understand a dream to tell what it means."

Joseph said, "It is not in me. God

shall give you an answer."

The king told Joseph both of his dreams. Joseph said, "The dream is one. God has showed you what He is soon going to do. The seven good cows and the seven good ears are seven years. The seven thin cows and the seven poor ears are seven years. First there will be seven very good years when there will be plenty to eat. After that there will be seven years of famine when there will not be enough to eat even with what was gathered in the seven good years."

Joseph said, "You dreamed twice because the dream is from God, and God will soon make it happen. Look for a wise man to be ruler over the land. Let him gather in much food in the seven good years and save it to eat when the seven years of famine come."

The king thought there was no one in his kingdom so wise as Joseph, for

God was with him. So he made Joseph ruler over all the land. He was greater than any other man in the land except the king. The king gave Joseph a woman to be his wife. They had two sons.

In the seven good years, Joseph gathered in much food and put it into houses to save for the seven poor years.

At last the seven good years were ended. Then came the seven years of famine. There was not only a famine in Egypt where Joseph was, but there was a famine in every land. The time came when people did not have enough to eat. They came to Joseph for food. Joseph opened the houses and sold food to the people.

Soon people from other lands were coming to Egypt to buy food.

# Joseph Sees His Brothers

Genesis 42:1-24

The famine was in all lands, so it was also in the land of Canaan where Joseph's father and brothers lived. They had poor crops and they began to run out of food. Israel heard that there was plenty of food in the land of Egypt. He told his sons to go down to Egypt to buy food so that they would not die.

Israel did not send Benjamin along because he was his youngest son. He was afraid something might happen to him. He had lost Joseph, and he did not want to lose Benjamin, too. So the ten brothers went down to Egypt.

Since Joseph was ruler over the land and gave food to the people, the

brothers came to Joseph and bowed
down to him. Joseph knew who they
were but they did not know him. He
remembered his dreams. Now his
brothers did bow down to him, but
they did not know they were bowing
to Joseph.

Joseph did not know whether his
brothers were sorry they had sold
him or not. He did not know whether
they still hated him or not. So he did
not tell them who he was, but he gave
them some tests to see whether he
could trust them. He asked them from
where they had come.

"From the land of Canaan to buy
food," they answered.

Joseph talked as if he did not
believe them. But they said, "We
all are one man's sons. We are true
men and we have come to buy food."
Still Joseph talked as though he did
not believe them.

"We are twelve brothers," they said, "the sons of one man in the land of Canaan. The youngest one is with his father, but the other one is not living."

Joseph told them he would test them to see whether they were true men. He told them that unless they brought their youngest brother along the next time they came down for food, they could not even see him. He made one of the brothers stay in prison in Egypt until the brothers would come back again.

## Lesson 23
# The Brothers Go Home
### Genesis 42:25-43:15

Joseph told his men to fill his brothers' sacks with corn*. The brothers paid for it, but Joseph had the money put back into their sacks when the brothers did not see it.

As the brothers were on their trip home, they needed to feed their animals. When one of the brothers opened his sack to get feed, he discovered the money in his sack. When he told his brothers about it, they were very much afraid. They said, "What is this that God has done to us?"

When they got back to the land of Canaan, they told their father all the

things that had happened to them.
They told about the brother who had
to stay in prison until they would take
Benjamin along down to Egypt.

When the other brothers emptied
their sacks, they discovered the
money in their sacks, too. This
made them and their father very
much afraid.

Israel felt very sad. He thought
Joseph was dead. Simeon had to stay
in Egypt, and now they said they must
take Benjamin along next time. What
if something should happen to Benjamin,
too?

But the brothers felt sure that
Benjamin would be safe with them.
One of them said, "Kill my two sons
if I do not bring Benjamin back to
you again."

But Israel said, "My son shall not
go down with you, for his brother is
dead. If something should happen to

him, you would bring down my gray
hair with sorrow to the grave."

The time came when the food was
almost gone. Israel said to his sons,
"Go again and buy us a little food."

One of the sons answered, "The
man said that we cannot see him
unless our brother is with us. If you
will send him with us, we will go and
buy food. If you do not send him along,
we will not go."

Israel knew they needed the food,
so he told them to go and take a
present for the man, money to buy
more corn, and the money they had
found in their sacks. Then he asked
God to help them so that the brother
in prison and Benjamin could come
back home again.

The brothers took the money, a
present, and Benjamin and went down
into the land of Egypt.

*An English term for grain.

# The Brothers Eat With Joseph

Genesis 43:16-34

When Joseph saw that Benjamin was with them, he told the ruler of his house to get ready because he wanted the men to eat with him at noon.

So the ruler brought the men to Joseph's house and got ready for them to eat with Joseph. The brothers were very much afraid to be brought into Joseph's house. They thought it might be because of the money in their sacks. Maybe Joseph thought they had stolen it. Was he planning to punish them and make them stay and be his servants? They came to one of Joseph's helpers and said, "Oh, sir, we came down the first time to buy corn, and when we opened our sacks,

we found money in them. We brought
it back again besides more money
to buy more food. We cannot tell who
put our money into our sacks."

The man was very kind to them
and told them not to be afraid. He
brought out to them their brother
who had been in prison. He fed their
animals and gave them water to wash
their feet.

When Joseph came home, they
brought him their present and
bowed down to him.

Joseph asked, "Is your father well,
the old man you talked about? Is he
still alive?"

They answered, "Your servant,
our father, is in good health. He
is still alive."

Joseph looked up and saw his
younger brother Benjamin. He
asked, "Is this your younger brother
whom you told me about?" He said

to Benjamin, "God be good to you, my son." Then Joseph hurried and left the room because he had to cry. He cried because he was very happy to see Benjamin, but he did not want anyone to see him cry. He washed his face and went out to them again.

When they sat down to eat, they were sitting in the order of their ages. The brothers could not understand how Joseph's helper knew how old they were.

The food was brought in, and Benjamin was given five times as much food as the others. Everyone ate and had a good time with Joseph.

# Joseph Tests His Brothers

Genesis 44:1-13

Joseph said to one of his helpers, "Fill the men's sacks with as much food as they can carry. Put every man's money back into the top of his sack and put my cup, the silver cup, into the top of Benjamin's sack."

The man did just as Joseph told him to do. The brothers did not know what he did.

The next morning, as soon as it was light, the men started home. Before they had gone very far, Joseph said to his helper, "Go, follow after the men; and when you come to them, ask them why they stole my silver cup after I had been so kind to them." So the man went after them and asked them about this thing.

The brothers said, "Why do you say that? We brought back the money that we found in our sacks before. Then why would we steal silver or gold? With whomever you find the silver cup, he can die, and we will be your master's servants." They said this because they knew they had not taken it. They had no idea it would be in Benjamin's sack.

This was another way Joseph tested his brothers. Would they be glad if something happened to Benjamin?

The man told them that only the man who had the silver cup would need to stay and be a servant. The others could go home.

Quickly the brothers took down their sacks, and each one opened his sack. The man looked into each sack, starting with the oldest brother's sack. It was not in the first sack. He looked in the next sack. It was not there. Last of all he looked into Benjamin's sack. There was the silver cup.

The poor brothers felt very sad. What would their poor father say if they went back home and Benjamin was not with them? Oh! what could they do? One of them had promised their father to bring Benjamin safely home. They were in great trouble. They loaded up their sacks and went back to talk to Joseph.

# Joseph Makes Himself Known
Genesis 44:14-45:3

Joseph was still in his house when the brothers got there. They fell on the ground in front of him. Joseph asked them, "What is this that you have done?"

The brother who promised to bring Benjamin back home was Judah. He said to Joseph, "What shall we say? We will be your servants, both we and the one who had the silver cup."

But Joseph said, "Just the one who had the silver cup will be my servant. The rest of you may go home to your father."

Judah came to Joseph and said, "Oh, let me speak a word to you, and do not be angry with us. You

asked us whether we have a father
or a brother. We told you that we
have a father who is an old man, a
little brother, and a dead brother.
The little brother is the only one left
of his mother's children, and his
father loves him. And you said we
should bring him down so that you
could see him. We said that he
cannot leave his father or his father
will die. And you said we could not
see you again unless we bring him
along. So when we went back to our
father, we told him what you said.
Our father told us to go again and buy
a little food. We told him that we
could not come unless Benjamin comes
along. He said that one of his sons is
gone, and if we take Benjamin along
and anything happens to him, he would
be in sorrow and die. Now if I do not
take Benjamin along back home, I am
afraid my father will die. I promised

to bring Benjamin back home.  Please
let me stay instead of Benjamin.  I
will be your servant.  Let the lad go
home to his father."

Now Joseph knew that his brothers
were not wicked anymore.  He told all
his helpers to go away from him.  He
wanted to be alone with his brothers.

When he was alone with them, he
began to cry.  He cried so loudly that
the people outside heard him.  Then
he said to his brothers, "I am Joseph."

The brothers were so afraid that
they did not know what to say.  Joseph
did not want his brothers to be afraid
of him.  He loved them even though
they had not been kind to him.  He
was not going to punish them.

# Good News for Israel

### Genesis 45:4-28

Joseph was very kind to his brothers
and told them to come near. They
came to him and he said, "I am
Joseph, your brother, whom you sold
into Egypt. Now do not be angry with
yourselves for selling me here. God
sent me here so that you would not
need to die. Already there have been
two years of famine, but there will
be five more years when you will not
have crops. God sent me here to save
your lives, and He made me ruler
over this land. Now hurry and go back
to my father. Tell him to come down
to me."

He told all his brothers to come
and bring their wives and children

down to Egypt to live. Then he would see to it that they had plenty to eat.

Joseph kissed Benjamin and all his other brothers and cried. After that his brothers talked to him.

Soon the news that these men were Joseph's brothers spread to the king and his servants. They were very happy about it and wanted them to come down to their land to live. The king told Joseph to give them plenty of food and clothes and wagons. Joseph sent a special present for his father.

Perhaps their father was eager to see whether they all would get home safely. Would Benjamin come back with them? He did not know what good news was coming!

When the brothers got home, they said, "Joseph is still alive! He is ruler over all the land of Egypt."

Their father could not believe it. But when they told him all the things

that Joseph had said and showed him
all the wagons he had sent along,
Israel believed them. He said,
"Joseph my son is still alive. I
will go and see him before I die."

# Israel Moves to Egypt

Genesis 46:1-50:26

Israel and his sons got ready to move to the land of Egypt. On the way they stopped. Israel offered an offering to God, and that night God talked to him. He told him not to be afraid to go down to Egypt where Joseph was. He said, "I will be with you and bring you back again."

Israel sent Judah ahead to show them the way to go. Joseph got ready and went out to meet his father. How glad they were to see each other again! They were so happy to see each other that they cried a long time. Israel said, "Now let me die, for I have seen you and you are still alive."

But Israel did not die right away. He lived near Joseph in the land of Egypt for seventeen years. Israel had had many troubles, but God was good to him.

Joseph went in to the king and told him that his father and brothers had moved down to Egypt. And do you know what the king told Joseph? He told Joseph to let them live in the best part of his land! So that is where Joseph had them live, and he saw to it that they had plenty to eat.

Before Israel died, he called his sons. He told them not to bury him in Egypt, but to take him back to Canaan to be buried. After he died, the brothers took him back to Canaan and buried him.

Now Joseph's brothers were afraid again. They thought that since their father was dead, Joseph might try to pay them back for what they had done.

But Joseph said, "Do not be afraid. You meant to do me harm, but God meant it for good. Because you sold me here, many people have been saved alive. Do not be afraid. I will feed you and your little ones."

The time came that Joseph knew he was soon going to die. He told his brothers that someday God would take them back to Canaan. He said that when they go, they should take his bones along and bury him there. He died when he was one hundred ten years old.

## Lesson 29

# Trouble for Job

Job 1:1-19

A long time ago there lived in the
land of Uz a good man who obeyed
God and always tried to do what was
right. He had a big family of seven
sons and three daughters. He was a
very rich man. He had seven thousand
sheep and three thousand camels,
besides many other animals.

This man's name was Job. Job wanted
all his sons and daughters to obey God.
He tried to help them do what was right.

Satan is the enemy of God and
man. He was not pleased that Job
loved and obeyed God. He thought
Job obeyed God because God was
so good to him. He thought if God
would take away the things He had

given to Job, Job would not like God anymore. So Satan talked to God about this. God told Satan he could take Job's things from him.

Job did not know what Satan thought or that Satan was going to take away his things to see whether he would hate God.

One day one of Job's servants came to Job and said that some men had come and taken his cattle and killed his servants. "I am the only one left to tell you," he said.

As he was telling this to Job, another servant came and said, "Some men took away your camels and killed the servants. I am the only one left to tell you."

While he was still speaking, another man came to Job. He had the worst news of all. He said, "Your children were eating in their oldest brother's house. A wind came and blew the house down on them and killed them. I am the only one left to tell you."

## Lesson 30

# Satan Tries Again

### Job 1:20-42:17

Now Job did not have his seven thousand sheep or his three thousand camels. He did not have his other animals. But worst of all, all his children had been killed. The wind had blown the house down on them while they were eating. This was much bad news for Job all in one day.

Job did not know why God let all his animals and children be taken away. But Job said, "The Lord gave and the Lord has taken away. Blessed be the Name of the Lord." So you see that Job did not do what Satan thought he would do and wanted him to do. He loved God even when all his animals and children were taken away from him.

Satan is a very bad enemy. He wanted to try again to make Job sin. He made Job have sore boils on his head, on his feet, and all over him! Poor Job! Even his wife thought he should hate God. But even with all this, Job would not sin. He was willing to take what God gave him.

Job had three friends who came to see him. They had heard that his children and animals were killed and that he had boils. So they came to see him. When they were still a long way off and saw poor Job, they cried. Then they came to Job and sat down with him. But they did not talk to him for seven days because they saw that Job was very sad.

The three friends thought that God had taken away Job's animals and children because he had sinned. They thought that God had given him boils to punish him. That made Job feel even worse. The friends should have helped him, but instead they made him feel worse.

God did not like what the three friends said to Job. He told them that they did not do what was right as Job did; so they should make an offering to God, and Job would pray for them.

The three friends gave an offering to God, and Job prayed for them. Then wonderful things happened. God took away Job's boils. He gave him twice as many animals as he had had before. He also gave him seven sons and three daughters again. God let Job live a long time after this.

# Unit 2

## Moses Leads
### God's People

# Bible Memory Verses

## The Ten Commandments
### Exodus 20:3-17

1. Thou shalt have no other gods before me.

2. Thou shalt not make unto thee any graven image.

3. Thou shalt not take the name of the Lord thy God in vain.

4. Remember the sabbath day, to keep it holy.

5. Honor thy father and thy mother.

6. Thou shalt not kill.

7. Thou shalt not commit adultery.

8. Thou shalt not steal.

9. Thou shalt not bear false witness against thy neighbor.

10. Thou shalt not covet.

# A Hard Time for God's People

Exodus 1

You remember that Joseph had been sold into the land of Egypt. The people who live in Egypt are dark-skinned people.

One time the people in Egypt had a new king. The king saw in his land some people who were not like his people. They were not dark people. There were really more of these people than there were of the dark-skinned people.

Do you know who these people were? They were called the children of Israel. When they first came to Egypt, many years before this, there were only seventy of them. They were Joseph's father, Israel, and his sons. You remember how they brought their families and came down to live in this land near Joseph. Now Joseph and all his brothers were dead, so these people were Israel's grandchildren or great grandchildren, or maybe even great great grandchildren, but they all were known as the children of Israel. At this time there were many thousands of them.

The king was afraid to have so many of these people in his land. He was afraid that sometime they might try to kill him and his people. He talked to his people about this. He said, "See, there are more of the children of Israel than there are of us. Come, let us try to keep them from becoming so strong."

So the king put masters over the children of Israel to make them work for the king. They made them work very, very hard. But the meaner they treated them, the more people there were. The people of Egypt did not like this. So they made their lives very unhappy with a lot of hard work. They were very mean to them. Whatever they had them do, it was very hard. If they made bricks, they had very hard work. If they worked in the field, it was very hard. There were many different kinds of work to do, and it was all very hard.

At last the king talked to two of the women who helped take care of the babies. He said, "If the baby is a boy, kill him. But if it is a baby girl, you may let it live."

These two women did not obey the king. They did not know whether or not the king would kill them if they did not obey him. But they knew God did not want them to kill the little babies. They wanted to obey God. So they saved all the little boy babies.

One day the king called for these women. He asked them, "Why have you saved the little boy babies?" God helped the women to give the king a good answer.

And God helped them so that the king did not hurt them. God was pleased that they would obey Him rather than obey the king.

But then the king told all the children of Israel, "You shall throw into the river every little boy that is born. But you may save all the little girls."

## Lesson 2

# The Baby in the Boat

Exodus 2:1-10

The Bible tells us that among the children of Israel there was a family who had a baby boy. It was at the time that the king had said all the baby boys should be thrown into the river. But this family was not afraid of what the king had said. They believed God would help them. They saw that their little baby was a very nice baby. So they hid him three months. By that time their baby was too old to be hidden anymore.

So his mother took a little boat and put pitch on it so that no water could get into it. Into this little boat she put her baby. Then she took the boat and put it in the flags near the side of the river.

This baby had an older sister whose

name was Miriam. She stood away from where the little boat was put. She wanted to see what would happen to her baby brother.

Some women came down to the river. One of these women was the princess. Her father was the king who had said that all the little boys should be killed. Would she see the little baby? She had come down to the river to wash herself. As she and the other women were walking along the side of the river, she saw something among the flags. What was it? Yes, it was the little boat. The princess sent one of the women to get it for her.

She opened the little boat and saw the baby in it. The poor little baby cried. The princess felt sorry for him. She knew it was one of the babies that her father had said should be killed. But she did not want him to be killed. She wanted to keep the baby.

Miriam came and asked the princess,

"Shall I get one of our women to take care of the child for you?"

The princess said, "Go."

So Miriam went and called her mother. When she came, the princess said, "Take this child and take care of him for me. I will pay you."

How happy the baby's mother must have been! Now she could take care of her little baby again without having to hide him. She took care of him and he grew. Then she took him to the princess, and he became her son. The princess called his name Moses. She took good care of him.

# Moses Runs Away

Exodus 2:11-25

God had a very special plan for Moses. He had saved his life for a very special reason. The children of Israel were having a hard time, and God cared for them. He wanted to help them get away from that king and bring them out of Egypt into a better land. He chose Moses to be the one to lead them out of Egypt. Moses seemed to know this. He thought that the children of Israel knew, too, that God was going to use him to help them, but they did not seem to understand.

One day when Moses was grown, he went out to visit his own people, the children of Israel. He saw that they had very hard work to do. It was very, very hard. Then he saw an Egyptian hitting one of the children of Israel. He looked all around him, but he did not see anyone. So he killed the Egyptian and hid him in the sand.

The next day Moses went out again. This time he saw two men of the children of Israel fighting. The one man hit the other one. Moses said to him, "Why did you hit him?"

He answered, "Who made you a ruler over us? Do you plan to kill me as you did the Egyptian yesterday?"

Then Moses was afraid. Someone knew that he had killed an Egyptian. If the king found this out, he would try to kill him. Sure enough, the king did find it out. He looked for Moses so that he could kill him. But Moses ran away from the king. He knew it was not safe to stay. He came to a different land and sat down by a well. While he was there, seven sisters came to get water for their father's flock.

Some men who took care of sheep came and made the sisters stay away. Moses stood up and helped the sisters and watered their flock for them.

When the sisters came back to their father, their father asked, "How did you get back so soon from watering your flock today?"

They said to their father, "A man from Egypt helped us and drew enough water for us and watered our flock."

Their father said, "Where is he? Why did you leave him? Call him so that he can eat bread with us."

Moses was glad to live with this man. His name was Jethro. Jethro gave Moses one of his daughters to be his wife. God gave them a little son.

After a time the king of Egypt died. But the children of Israel still had a hard time. They cried to God, and God heard them. He would get Moses ready to go back to them and take them out of Egypt.

## Lesson 4

# Moses Sees Something Strange

Exodus 3:1-4:9

Moses took care of a flock of sheep for his wife's father. One day he came to a mountain called "The Mountain of God." There Moses saw something very strange. He saw a bush that was burning with fire, but the bush did not burn up!

Moses turned to see why the fire did not destroy the bush. When God saw that he turned to look at the bush, God called to him from the middle of the bush. He said, "Moses, Moses."

"Here I am," answered Moses.

God said, "Do not come near. Take your shoes off your feet because the place where you are standing is holy ground. I am the God of your father, the God of Abraham, the God of Isaac, and the God of Jacob."

Moses hid his face because he was afraid to look at God. Then God told Moses that He had seen all the hard things that His people in Egypt were going through and that He had come down to bring them out of Egypt into a better land. He wanted to bring them back to the land of Canaan. God said, "Come, and I will send you to bring My people, the children of Israel, out of Egypt."

Moses did not feel that he would be able to do this. He asked God, "Who am I, that I should bring the children of Israel out of Egypt?"

God said, "I will be with you. When you bring the people out of Egypt, you will worship Me on this mountain. Go and gather together the older men of Israel and tell them that I see what they are going through, and I will bring them out of the land of Egypt into a very good land. They will listen to what you say.

Then you and the older men shall go in to the king and ask him to let you go on a three-day trip to sacrifice to God. But I am sure the king will not let you go. Then I will do all My wonders, and after that he will let you go."

Moses was still afraid to go. He thought the people would not listen to him or believe what he said. The Lord said, "What is that in your hand?"

"A rod," answered Moses.

God said, "Throw it on the ground." So Moses threw it on the ground. The rod turned into a snake, and Moses ran away from it. God said, "Put out your hand and take it by the tail." Moses put out his hand and took it by the tail. Then it became a rod in his hand again.

God told him to put his hand inside his clothes. Moses did, and when he took his hand out again, it had on it a disease which made it white. God told him to put his hand in again. So he did and when he took it out, his hand was well again like the other one.

God made Moses able to do these things so that he could show them to His people in Egypt. Then they would know God was with him and believe what he said.

God told Moses that if they still did not believe when he showed them these two wonders, he should take some water out of the river and put it on the ground. Then it would turn into blood.

# Moses Goes Back to Egypt

Exodus 4:10-31

Even after God had given Moses all these wonders to show to the people in Egypt, Moses seemed to be afraid to go. He told the Lord that he could not talk well enough.

But God said, "Who made man's mouth? Who makes people so that they cannot speak, or so that they are deaf or blind, or so that they can see? Have not I? Now go and I will be with you and tell you what to say."

Even then Moses did not want to go. He wanted someone else to go and do the talking for him. This did not please God. God had promised to help him, and He wanted Moses to believe Him and be willing to do as he was told to do.

126

God said, "Is not Aaron your brother? I know that he can speak well. He is coming to meet you, and he will be happy to see you. You can tell him what to say, and he can talk to the people. Take this rod in your hand so that you can do those wonders."

Moses went to his father-in-law, Jethro. He said, "Please let me go back to my people who are in Egypt and see whether they are still alive."

Jethro told Moses that he could go. God also told Moses to go, because by this time all the people who wanted to kill him were dead. Moses took his wife and their two sons and the rod in his hand and started back to the land of Egypt.

God again told Moses that the king would not let the people go out of Egypt. He told him to tell the king that if he would not let the people go, God would kill his oldest boy.

God said to Aaron, Moses' older

brother, "You go out to meet Moses." Aaron went and met him at the Mountain of God. This was the mountain where Moses saw the burning bush that did not burn up. Moses told Aaron all about what God had told him and about the wonders that God had given him to show in Egypt.

Moses and Aaron went to Egypt and gathered together the older men of the children of Israel. They told them that the Lord had sent Moses and Aaron to bring them out of Egypt into a better land. They showed them the wonders that God had given them. The children of Israel believed what Moses and Aaron said and were very glad that God had seen what trouble they were in and that He was going to help them. They bowed their heads and thanked the Lord.

## Lesson 6
# More Trouble for God's People
### Exodus 5:1-6:1

After Moses and Aaron had talked to the children of Israel, they went to talk to the king of Egypt. He was called Pharaoh. They told him that the Lord said he should let His people go.

But King Pharaoh said, "Who is the Lord, that I should obey Him? I do not know the Lord, and I will not let Israel go."

But Moses and Aaron said, "Our God has met with us. Please let us take a three-day trip to sacrifice to our God or something bad might happen to us."

"Why do you, Moses and Aaron, keep the people from their work?" asked King Pharaoh. "There are many people and you let them rest from their work."

That same day the king said to the men who made God's people work too hard, "Do not give the people straw to make brick as you have been doing. Have them go and get the straw themselves. Yet with this extra work, be sure they still make as many bricks as they made before. They are just lazy. That is why they want to go and sacrifice to the Lord. Give them more work to do."

So these men went out to the people and said, "The king says that he will not give you straw. Go get the straw wherever you can find it. But you still must get just as much work done as you did before."

Before this the children of Israel had to work very hard and now they would have to do more work yet. They just could not do all the work that they were asked to do. When they did not get all the work done, their masters beat them and scolded them. Now they were in worse trouble than before Moses and Aaron had come. They could not understand why Moses and Aaron had said they were going to help them and now things were worse instead of better.

Some of the men went to talk to the king about the trouble they were in. They said, "Why do you do this to us? They do not give us straw anymore, and yet they want us to make as many bricks as before. Then they beat us, and it is your people's fault."

But King Pharaoh said, "You are lazy and that is why you want to go and sacrifice to the Lord. Go now and get to work because we will not give you any straw, and yet you still must make as many bricks as you did before."

When the men saw that it did no good to talk to the king, they left. On the way out, they met Moses and Aaron. They told them about the new trouble they were having. Moses asked the Lord about it.

He said, "Lord, why have You let all this come on Your people, and why did You send me? Since I came to the king to talk to him, he has made it harder for the people; and You have not helped us at all."

The Lord answered Moses, "You will see what I will do to the king. He will drive you out of his land."

# The First Wonder

Exodus 6:9-7:24

The Lord told Moses what to tell the children of Israel now while they were being treated so meanly by the people of Egypt. He told Moses to say to them, "I am the Lord, and I will bring you out of your burdens. I will take you to be My people, and I will be your God. You will know that I am the Lord. I will bring you into the land that I promised Abraham, Isaac, and Jacob would be given to you. I will give you this land."

Moses went and told the children of Israel these things. But they were being treated so badly and were suffering so much that they did not listen to him.

The Lord told Moses to go in and talk to the king so that he would let the children of Israel go. But Moses said to God, "The children of Israel have not listened to me. How then will the king listen to me?"

But God told him to go. So Moses and Aaron went in to the king. They took along the rod as God had told them to do. When they were there before the king, Aaron threw down his rod, and it turned into a snake. Then the king called in his magicians. They threw down their rods, and they became snakes, too. But Aaron's rod swallowed up their rods. The king still would not believe God or let the children of Israel go.

Then the Lord said to Moses, "The king still will not let the people go. In the morning the king will go down to the river. You be down there when he comes. Take along with you in your hand the rod that was turned into a snake. You tell the king that your God has sent you to him to tell him to let you go. Tell him that he will know that I am the Lord. And tell him that you will hit the water with the rod that is in your hand, and the water in the river will turn into blood. The fish that are in the river will die, and the river will stink. They will hate to drink of the water."

Moses and Aaron went down to the river. While King Pharaoh and his servants were watching, Aaron hit the river with his rod, and all the waters were turned into blood. The king's magicians did the same thing with their rods. The fish could not live in the blood, so they all died. Then there was a terrible stink because of all the blood and the dead fish.

But still this did not make the king let the children of Israel go out of his land. The people of Egypt dug around by the river to try to find water to drink. They could not drink the water of the river because it had been turned into blood.

# Frogs in Egypt

Exodus 7:25-8:15

Seven days went by after God had made the water in the river turn into blood. Then the Lord talked to Moses again. He said, "Go to the king and tell him that I said he should let My people go that they may serve Me. If he will not let them go, I will bring frogs into his land. There will be many frogs in the river, and they will come up into his house. They will come into the houses of his servants and into the houses of all his people. They will come into the ovens and into the places where they make bread. They will be on him and on all his servants and all his people."

The king still would not let the people go, so God told Moses to tell Aaron to put his rod out over the rivers so that frogs would come up on the land of Egypt. Aaron put his rod out over the water, and frogs came up and covered the land of Egypt. Pharaoh's magicians also brought frogs over the land of Egypt.

Can you think how terrible it would be to have frogs all over your things? You know how frogs can jump. How would you like to have frogs jumping on you and all over your house and into your food? Well, the king did not like it, either. He called for Moses and Aaron and told them to ask the Lord to take away the frogs from him and his people. He said he would let the people go so that they could sacrifice to the Lord.

Moses asked the king, "When shall I ask that all the frogs be destroyed from you and your houses and that they stay only in the river?"

"Tomorrow," answered the king.

Moses said, "It will be just as you

said so that you can know there is no one like our God. The frogs shall go away from you and your houses and from your servants and your people. They will stay only in the river."

Moses and Aaron went out from the king, and Moses asked the Lord to take away the frogs. The Lord did as Moses asked, and all the frogs in the houses and towns and fields died. The people gathered the dead frogs together on big piles. Then the land did stink.

When the king saw that the frogs were gone, he would not let the children of Israel go as he had said he would.

Lesson 9

# Lice and Flies

Exodus 8:16-32

The Lord said to Moses, "Tell Aaron to put out his rod and hit the dust of the land so that it will become lice in all the land of Egypt." So Aaron put out his rod and hit the dust of the earth, and it became lice. The dust on the people became lice, and the dust on the animals became lice. The king's magicians tried to bring lice as Aaron had done, but they could not. So they knew that this was from God. They told the king that this was from God, but even then the king would not let the people go.

The Lord said to Moses, "Get up early in the morning and come to the king as he comes out to the water. Tell him that the Lord says he is to let My people go so that they can serve Me. If he will not let them go, I will send swarms of flies on him and his servants and on all his people. Their houses will be full of flies, and the ground will be full of flies. But there will not be flies in the land where My people live, so that he may know that I am the Lord."

The Lord brought a terrible swarm of flies into the house of the king, into the houses of his servants, and into all the land of Egypt.

King Pharaoh called for Moses and Aaron. He said, "You go and sacrifice to your God here in the land."

Moses told him this would not be the thing to do. He said they must go on a three-day trip as the Lord told them to do.

The king said, "I will let you go so that you can sacrifice to the Lord, but do not go very far away."

Moses said, "I will go and ask the

Lord to take away the swarms of flies from the king and his servants and all his people tomorrow. But do not change your mind and say you will let us go and then not do it."

Moses went out from the king and asked the Lord to take away the flies. The Lord took away all the flies from the king and from his servants and from all the people. There was not one fly left.

When all the flies were gone, the king did just as he had done before. He would not let the children of Israel go.

# More Terrible Wonders

Exodus 9:1-12

The Lord said to Moses, "Go to the king and tell him that the Lord says he must let My people go so that they may serve Me. Tell him that if he will not let them go, the Lord will bring a very bad disease on the animals of his people. It will be on the cows, the horses, the donkeys, the camels, the oxen, and the sheep. It will be terrible. But nothing will die of the animals that belong to My people, Israel. Tomorrow I will do this thing."

The next day the Lord did as He had said. All the cattle in Egypt died, but none of the cattle of the children of Israel died. The king sent someone to look, and they did not find dead any of the cattle of

the children of Israel. But even with this, the king still would not let the people go.

The Lord said to Moses and Aaron, "Take from the stove handfuls of ashes and let Moses sprinkle them toward heaven while the king is watching. The ashes will become small dust in all the land of Egypt and will break out as boils on all the men and animals in the land of Egypt."

Moses and Aaron took ashes from the stove and stood by the king. They sprinkled the ashes up toward heaven, and they became boils breaking out on the men and on the animals.

The magicians could not stand before Moses because of the boils. The boils were upon the magicians and upon all the Egyptians. But King Pharaoh still would not let the people go.

## Lesson 11

# Thunder, Lightning, and Hail

Exodus 9:13-35

The Lord said to Moses, "Get up early in the morning and stand before the king and tell him that this is what the Lord says: 'Let My people go that they may serve Me. I will at this time send all My troubles on you and your servants and on all your people so that you will know that there is no one like Me in all the earth. Tomorrow about this time I will make it rain a terrible hail such as there has never been before in the land of Egypt. So now, send some men to gather in your cattle and all that you have in the field. Every person and animal that is not brought home will be hit by the hail and will die.' "

Some of the king's servants believed

what Moses said, and they were afraid.
These servants made all their servants
and animals get into houses so that they
would not be hurt by the hail.

Some of the king's servants did not
believe what Moses said, and they were
not afraid. They left their servants and
animals out in the field.

The Lord told Moses to put out his
hand toward heaven so that there would be
hail on the men and animals and plants in
all the land of Egypt. Moses put out his
rod toward heaven. The Lord sent thunder and hail, and fire ran along the
ground. Fire was mixed in with the hail,
very terrible. The people in Egypt had
never seen anything like it. It killed the
men and the animals that were left outside, and it broke down all the trees. It
spoiled their flax and their barley. But
in the part of the land where the children
of Israel lived, there was no hail.

King Pharaoh called for Moses and

Aaron. He said, "I have sinned this time. The Lord is good, but I and my people are wicked. Ask the Lord that there be no more mighty thunderings and hail. I will let you go. You do not need to stay any longer."

Moses said, "As soon as I am out of the city, I will spread out my hands to the Lord. The thunder will stop, and there will not be any more hail so that you can know that the earth belongs to the Lord."

Moses went out of the city and spread out his hands to the Lord. The thunder and hail stopped and there was no more rain.

But when the king saw that the rain and thunder and hail had stopped, he still would not let the people go.

## Lesson 12

## Locusts

Exodus 10:1-20

The Lord said to Moses, "Go in to the king again. I have made his heart hard so that I can show all My signs to him. Then you can tell your children and your grandchildren about all these things that I have done so that you may know that I am the Lord."

Just think! Now you are reading the same stories which the children of Israel told to their children and their grandchildren. Their fathers told them the stories of how the water was turned to blood. They heard about the frogs and lice and the flies. They were told about the terrible disease the Egyptian cattle had and how they died, but how none of their cattle had that disease. They were told about the terrible thunder and hail and fire. They knew that their God was a great God and that He could do great things for them.

Moses and Aaron came in to the king and said, "God says, 'How long will you be like this? Let My people go. But if you will not let them go, tomorrow I will bring locusts. These locusts will cover the earth so thickly that you will not be able to see the earth. They will eat all the crops that the hail did not spoil. They will fill your houses and the houses of your servants and of all your people. It will be worse than it ever was before in the land.' " After Moses had warned the king, he and Aaron turned and went out.

After Moses and Aaron were gone, the king's servants said to the king, "How long will this man bother us? Let the men go to serve their God. Don't you know that Egypt will be destroyed?"

King Pharaoh called for Moses and

Aaron to come back again. He said, "Go serve the Lord. But how many of you will go?"

Moses told him that they all would go. The old people would go. The young people would go. The boys and girls would go. Even their animals would go with them.

But the king did not want them all to go. Moses and Aaron were driven away from the king. Then the Lord said to Moses, "Stretch out your hand over the land of Egypt so that the locusts may come up on the land and eat everything that the hail left."

Moses stretched out his rod over the land of Egypt, and the Lord brought an east wind on the land all day and all night. When the morning came, the east wind brought the locusts. There had never been locusts like this before, and there never will be locusts like this again. They covered the earth so thickly that it was dark even in the daytime. They ate every green thing that was left.

This was terrible. The king hurried and called for Moses and Aaron. He said, "I have sinned against the Lord and against you. Please forgive me and ask the Lord to take these locusts away."

Moses went out and asked the Lord to take away the locusts. The Lord made a great west wind blow. It took away all the locusts into the Red Sea. Not one locust was left in Egypt. But when the king saw that the locusts were gone, he would not let the people go.

Lesson 13

# The Thick Darkness

Exodus 10:21-11:10

The Lord said to Moses, "Stretch out your hand toward heaven so that it will be dark over all the land of Egypt. It will be so dark that the darkness will be felt."

Moses stretched out his hand toward heaven, and a thick darkness came over the land of Egypt. It lasted three days. The people could not see each other, and they did not try to move around. They just stayed where they were for three days. It was not dark like this in the part of the land where the children of Israel lived. There was light where they lived.

King Pharaoh called for Moses and said, "You go, and serve the Lord, but do not take your flocks and your herds. You may take your children along with you."

But Moses said, "We must take our cattle along with us. We must use them to serve the Lord. We will not leave one behind because we do not know which ones the Lord wants until we get there."

The king did not like this, so he would not let them go. He said to Moses, "You get away and be careful that you do not see me any more, because on the day that you see me you are going to die."

Moses said, "What you have said is true. I will see your face no more."

The Lord told Moses that He would bring one more terrible thing on the king and on Egypt, and after that the king would let them go.

The Lord told Moses to tell the children of Israel to borrow things from the people of Egypt who were their neighbors. God caused the people of Egypt to treat the children of Israel kindly and to be glad to give them the things they asked to borrow. Also,

Moses was very great in the sight of the Egyptians.

The Lord told Moses about the last terrible thing that He would bring on the people of Egypt. Moses told King Pharaoh, "About midnight the Lord will go through Egypt, and all the firstborn sons will die." That means the oldest sons of all Pharaoh's people would die. Even the firstborn of the animals would have to die. God said there would be a terrible cry in the land of Egypt as there has never been before or ever will be again. After that the king would be glad to let them go, for fear that a more terrible thing might happen.

You remember that the king thought he did not have to obey the Lord, but he was going to find out how terrible it is not to obey the Lord. The people of Israel would not be hurt because they obeyed the Lord. Their firstborn sons would not need to die.

## Lesson 14
# What Happened at Midnight
Exodus 12:1-33

The Lord had some very special plans for the children of Israel for the last night they would spend in Egypt. He told them just what He wanted them to do, and He wanted them to do just what He said. This would be their last night in the land where they had to work so hard and were beaten. God had said that He would bring them out and now He was ready to do it.

This is what God wanted them to do. On the tenth day of that month the people of each house were to take a lamb. Each house was to take only one lamb, but if there were not enough people in one house to eat a whole lamb, they could invite their neighbors over and eat it together. There was not to be anything wrong with the lamb, and it was not to be over one year old.

They were to keep the lamb until the fourteenth day of the month. In the evening of that day the people of each house were to kill their lamb. Then they were to take its blood and sprinkle it on the side posts of their door and on the post above the door of their house. In the night they were to eat the lamb with bitter plants and with bread that had no yeast in it. They were to eat every part of the lamb and not leave any part of it. If any was left, the next morning they were to burn it with fire. Everyone was to stay in the house. No one was to go outside until the morning.

That night the Lord was going to go through Egypt and kill all the firstborn sons. But wherever He saw blood above the door, He would pass over that house and not kill the firstborn son there. So you can see how important it was for the people of each house to obey God and kill a lamb and put the blood at the top and at the sides of their door. If they did not do that, their firstborn son would be killed.

When the children of Israel heard all these things, they bowed their heads and thanked the Lord. Then they went away and did what Moses and Aaron told them to do.

That night the Lord went through the land of Egypt and killed all the firstborn sons. King Pharaoh and all his servants got up in the night. All the people in Egypt got up, and there was a terrible cry in Egypt because there was someone dead in every house. King Pharaoh quickly called for Moses and Aaron and told them to go and serve the Lord. The Egyptians tried to get the children of Israel to leave quickly because they were afraid the Lord would kill all of them.

Lesson 15

# The People Leave Egypt

Exodus 12:34-14:5

The children of Israel borrowed gold and silver and clothes from the people of Egypt. The Lord made the people of Egypt gladly give them all these things. Besides this they took their bread dough and went up out of the land of Egypt. It is hard for us to think how many people went out of Egypt that night. There were probably more than a million people because the Bible says there were over one-half million men.

It had been many years since Israel and his family had moved down to Egypt. But do you remember that Joseph knew then that God would sometime take them out of Egypt? Joseph had told them that when they go back to the land of Canaan, they were to take his bones along. So now after many years, when the children of Israel were leaving, Moses took the bones of Joseph along with them.

God wanted His people always to remember about the night when He brought them out of Egypt. He wanted them to be sure to tell their children about that night and help them always to remember it. On the fourteenth day of that month they were always to kill a lamb and eat it with bitter plants and with bread that had no yeast in it. This would help them to remember the wonderful night in which the Lord had brought them out of Egypt.

The Lord had a very special way of leading the children of Israel in the way He wanted them to go. In the daytime He had a cloud for them to follow. In the nighttime, when they could not see a cloud so well, He had a pillar of fire for them to follow. Whenever the cloud or fire moved, the people moved. But when the cloud or fire stopped, the people stopped, too. The Lord led them to a sea called the Red Sea where they would stay awhile.

Now after the king heard that all the people were gone, he decided that he would go after them. These people had done a lot of work for him and he missed them. He thought they could not very easily get away from him. It looked as though they could not get away because they were by the sea. But the king forgot that they had a great God. God knew that the king would go after them, and He had a special reason for wanting them there by the sea when the king came after them.

Lesson 16

# God Helps His People

Exodus 14:6-22

The king got his own chariot ready to go. He also took six hundred of his best chariots, besides all the other chariots in Egypt, and started after the children of Israel. Each chariot had a captain, and besides the captains and chariots, there were many horses and many people. They came near the children of Israel who were camping by the Red Sea.

When the children of Israel looked up and saw the Egyptians coming after them, they were very much afraid. They were afraid they were going to be killed. They scolded Moses for bringing them out of Egypt. They thought it would have been better for them to stay and work for the people in Egypt than to be brought to this place to die.

But Moses said to the people, "Do not be afraid. Stand still and see how the Lord will save you. The people of Egypt whom you see today you will never see again. The Lord will fight for you, and you shall be quiet."

The Lord told Moses to have the children of Israel move forward. Now if the children of Israel moved forward, they would go right into the Red Sea and the sea was too deep for them to cross. But God had a special way for them to get across. He told Moses to lift up his rod and stretch his hand out over the sea. Then the sea would divide, and the people could go over on dry land.

That night the angel of God went behind the children of Israel instead of going in front of them. And the pillar of cloud went behind them instead of going in front of them. In this way it was between the children of Israel and the people of Egypt. This cloud gave light to the children of Israel. They could see where to go. But it was very dark for the people of Egypt. Because of this they could not come near the children of Israel all night.

Moses stretched out his hand over the sea. Then the Lord made a strong wind blow that made the waters go back. It made a place of dry ground for the children of Israel to walk through. The water made a wall for them on their right side and on the left side, but in the place where they walked it was dry.

# What Happened to the People of Egypt

Exodus 14:23-15:27

When the people of Egypt got to the Red Sea, they also started through on this dry path. All the horses, all the chariots, and all the people went right into the middle of the sea. But you remember that the Lord had said He was going to fight for Israel, and He did. He took the wheels off the chariots of the people of Egypt. Now you know it would be very hard for horses to pull a chariot without any wheels. When the people saw that the wheels of the chariots were off, they were afraid. They said, "Let us run away from Israel because the Lord is fighting for them." But they could not get away very fast without any wheels on their chariots.

The Lord said to Moses, "Stretch out your hand over the sea so that the water may go back on the people of Egypt and on their chariots."

In the morning Moses stretched out his hand over the sea, and the sea came back. The people of Egypt tried to run to get out of the water, but they could not get out. The water covered the horses and chariots and all the people. Not one of them got out of the sea alive! When the children of Israel looked back, they saw many dead people on the seashore. They could never again hurt the children of Israel.

When the children of Israel saw what a wonderful thing the Lord had done for them, they believed that God was with them and that what Moses had done was the right thing. They were so happy that they sang a long song about this wonderful thing the Lord had done for them. They knew their God was the true God and that none of the gods or idols of the other people around them could do the things their God could do. The people around them would hear this wonderful story about how the Lord did fight for them. Then they would be afraid to try to fight with them and they could go on to the land that God had promised to give them.

The children of Israel traveled three days but they could not find any water. At last they came to a place where there was water, but they could not drink it because it was bitter. They grumbled to Moses and said, "What shall we drink?" They should not have grumbled to Moses. He could not help that the water was bitter. They should not have grumbled at all. The Lord would take care of them.

Moses talked to the Lord about it, and the Lord showed him a tree. Moses took this tree and threw it into the bitter water, and the water became sweet.

Then they had good water to drink.

The Lord promised them there that if they would always listen to Him and obey Him, He would keep them healthy.

After this they came to a place where there were twelve wells of water and seventy palm trees. They camped there by the water.

## Lesson 18

# God Feeds His People

Exodus 16:1-19

After a while the people left the place where there were twelve wells of water and seventy palm trees and came to a desert place. Now the children of Israel grumbled again. This time it was not that they did not have water. They grumbled because they wanted something to eat. They wished they were back in Egypt where they had plenty to eat.

It was wrong for them to wish a thing like that. God had been so good to them to bring them out of Egypt, and He would always take care of them if they would believe Him. It was true that there were many people to feed and they would not always know how to get enough food, but God always has a way to take care of His people.

He had a very special way of feeding them at this time. They were not able to raise crops because they were traveling. They would not be able to find enough wild animals to eat, so God made bread rain down from heaven for them. You never saw that kind of rain, did you? Every morning for six days God sent them bread from heaven. They were supposed to go out and gather all they would need for only one day and no more because God was going to send them new bread each day.

But the sixth day was different. On that day they were supposed to gather enough to last them for the seventh day. This was their Sabbath Day, or the day in which they were supposed to rest. God would not send them bread on the seventh day. They were to eat what they had gathered on the sixth day.

In the evening God sent them meat to

eat. He sent quails which covered the camp. Then the people could kill the quails and eat them.

In the morning when the children of Israel looked out on the ground, they saw a small white thing. They did not know what it was. Moses told them that it was bread God had sent them from heaven. The people did not know what this bread was, so they called it manna. After the sun came out, the manna that was left on the ground melted. Then the ground was ready for new manna the next morning. The manna was white and tasted very good. It tasted like wafers made with honey.

Moses told the people that God wanted them to gather each day only what they could eat and not leave any for the next day. On the sixth day they were to gather enough to last for the seventh day, which was their Sabbath Day of rest.

# God Gives Water to His People

Exodus 16:16-17:7

Do you know what kind of homes the children of Israel had to live in while they were traveling? They lived in tents. When they were ready to travel, they would take down their tents and carry them to the place where they were supposed to camp. Then they would put up their tents again. Of course, some families were larger than other families. The larger families would need more to eat than the smaller families. So some families gathered more manna each day than others. But each family was to gather only what their family could eat. The mothers did not need to decide what to have for breakfast or what to have for supper, because every morning they baked manna and every evening they had quail. For forty years the children of Israel traveled and for forty years they ate manna.

Some of the people did not obey Moses. They gathered more manna than they needed for one day and kept it overnight. The next morning it had worms in it and stank. Moses was angry with them for doing this. Some of them did not gather any extra manna on the sixth day to use on the seventh day. When they went out to gather manna on the seventh day, they could not find any. The Lord felt sorry that these people would not obey what He said they should do. He had been very good to them.

After a while the children of Israel again came to a place where there was no water to drink. They scolded Moses for this. They said, "Give us water so that we can drink."

Moses asked them, "Why do you scold

me?" Poor Moses could not help that there was no water to drink.

The people grumbled more. They said, "Why have you brought us up out of Egypt to kill us and our children and our cattle with thirst?"

Moses said to the Lord, "What shall I do to this people? They are almost ready to stone me."

The Lord said to Moses, "Go ahead of the people and take with you some of the older men of Israel. Take with you the rod that you used to hit the river. I will stand before you on a rock. You shall hit the rock and water will come out of it for the people to drink."

Moses did this, and water came out of the rock as the Lord had said.

## Lesson 20

# God Fights for His People

Exodus 17:8-18:27

While the people were camping at the place where they had gotten water to drink out of the rock, some men came out to fight with them.

Moses called Joshua to him and said, "Choose men and go out to fight with them. Tomorrow I will stand on the top of the hill with the rod of God in my hand."

Joshua chose men and went out to fight with the enemy. Moses and Aaron and Hur went up to the top of the hill. When Moses held up his hand, Israel was stronger, but when he let down his hand, the other people were stronger. It was hard for Moses to hold up his hands so long. They became very heavy. Aaron

and Hur took a stone and put it under Moses so that he could sit on it. Hur went on one side of Moses and held up one of his hands, and Aaron went on the other side and held up his other hand. They held Moses' hands up all the time until the sun went down. Then Israel was able to win. They killed the people who had come out to fight with them.

After this Moses built an altar to God.

When Jethro, Moses' father-in-law, heard about all the wonderful things that God had done for Israel, he came out to Moses in the desert. Moses went out to meet him, and they came into the tent for a visit. Moses told him about all the things that the Lord had done to the king in Egypt and about the troubles they had since they were traveling. He told about how the Lord had helped them in all their troubles.

Jethro was very happy to hear all these wonderful things. He said, "Now

I know that the Lord is greater than all gods." Then Jethro worshiped God.

The next day Moses sat down. From morning until evening he listened to the people as they came to him for help to know what they should do. Jethro thought it was not good for Moses to do this all day long. He thought this was too hard for him. He told Moses that he should choose good men to help him in this great work. Moses listened to his father-in-law and did what he told him to do. He chose men to help him with his work. Then Moses did not need to do all the work himself.

After this Jethro went back to his own land again.

## Lesson 21
# How God Speaks to His People
Exodus 19

After the children of Israel had been
in this place for a while, they took up
their tents and started to travel again.
At last they came to Mount Sinai, and
there they camped. This was the same
Mountain of God where Moses had been
when he saw the bush that was on fire
but did not burn up. They were going to
be at this place a long time.

Moses went up to God. God talked to
him from the mountain and said, "This
is what you shall tell the children of
Israel, 'You have seen what I did to the
people in Egypt and how I brought you to
Myself. Now if you will obey Me and do
what I tell you to do, then you will be
a treasure to Me more than any other

people on the earth.' "

Moses came down again and called the people and told them what the Lord had said. The people answered, "All that the Lord says we will do." Moses went back and told the Lord what the people said.

The Lord told Moses that He would come down in a thick cloud and talk to him so that all the people could hear. But the people would need to get ready for this. They must be clean from sin, and they must wash their clothes. Also God said that they must be careful not to go up to the mountain or even touch the edge of it because if they did they would die. Even if an animal touched the mountain it would die. So Moses went and told the people what the Lord had said and helped them to get ready for God to talk to them. In three days He would speak to them.

In the morning of the third day there were thunderings and lightnings, and a thick cloud was on the mountain. They heard a trumpet blow very loudly. It made the people shake with fear. Then the mountain began to smoke because God had come down upon it in fire. Then the mountain began to move. When the trumpet blew louder and louder, Moses called to the Lord, and the Lord answered Moses and told him to come up on the mountain. He told him to go down and warn the people again not to come up on the mountain or they would die. Only Moses and Aaron could come up on the mountain.

Moses went down to warn the people again. God always does His part to give plenty of warning to people. The sad part is that so many people do not obey even when they have had the warnings.

# The First Four Commandments

Exodus 20:1-11

It was here on Mount Sinai that God gave the ten commandments. A commandment is something that we are told to do. Wherever we are, we need rules. If we did not have any rules, the world would be a very unhappy place in which to live. God has given us rules to live by for our own good. We should be happy for good rules and try to keep them. We are sad and we make other people sad when we do not obey the rules. Would you like to hear the ten rules God gave to His people? In this lesson you will read about the first four commandments.

1. Thou shalt have no other gods before Me.

Many of the people in the countries

around the children of Israel did not love the true God. They worshiped other gods. We must not love other gods or worship them. We must love only God. If we love anything more than we love God, or if anything keeps us from loving God as we should, we are not keeping the first commandment that God gave to His people.

2. Thou shalt not make unto thee any graven image.

An image is something made to look like a real thing. It is often made of wood or stone or silver or gold. A cow made of wood is the image of a cow. Many people of the world worship idols or graven images. God did not want His people to make any images to be worshiped and served. They were to worship Him only.

3. Thou shalt not take the Name of the Lord thy God in vain.

God wanted His people, the children of

Israel, always to speak the truth. They were never to tell a lie and then use God's Name to try to make people believe that what they were saying was true.

4. Remember the Sabbath Day, to keep it holy.

The seventh day was the Sabbath Day for the children of Israel. On that day they were not to do any work that could be done other days. It was a special day to worship God, although they were to worship and be careful to please God every day. Doing nice things for others is one way to please God.

## Lesson 23

# The Last Six Commandments

Exodus 20:12-17

The first four of the ten commandments tell us how we should think about God and worship Him. The last six commandments tell us how we should treat one another. We will see what these six commandments are.

5. Honor thy father and thy mother.

Do you know what it means to honor someone? If we honor our fathers and mothers, we try to obey them and please them in every way we can because we love them. It is very important to God that we obey our parents. If we learn to love to obey them, we will not find it so hard to learn to obey and please God. God is pleased when children love and obey their parents.

6. Thou shalt not kill.

If we love people, we will not want to kill them. It is when people hate that they most often kill. We should be very careful not to hate anyone. God can help us to love even the people who are not nice to us.

7. Thou shalt not commit adultery.

When someone gets married, she or he is supposed to live with that man or woman as long as they both live. But if one of them leaves and the man lives with another woman or the woman lives with another man, they are doing what this commandment tells them not to do.

8. Thou shalt not steal.

To steal is to take something that belongs to someone else. If we love other people, we will not take their things away from them. If we have ever stolen anything, we should try to give back whatever we have taken and be sure never to steal again.

9. Thou shalt not bear false witness against thy neighbor.

To bear false witness is to say things that are not true. We should not tell lies about others. Even if we think something is true but we are not sure, we should be careful not to say it.

10. Thou shalt not covet.

To covet is to want something that does not belong to us and that we should not have. God knows what is best for us. He may not want us to have what He has given to others. We should not want things just because someone else has them. God wants us to be happy with the things He has given to us and not wish for the things He has given to others.

# How the People Worshiped God

Exodus 20:18-31:18

The people were afraid to have God talk to them. They said to Moses, "You talk to us and we will listen. But do not let God talk to us or we might die."

Moses said to the people, "Do not be afraid. God has come so that you will be afraid to sin." We do not need to be afraid if we obey God, but we need to be afraid if we do not obey God.

Moses again went up into the mountain where God was. It was very dark up there. Moses was there on the mountain forty days and forty nights.

God had many things to tell Moses. He wanted the children of Israel to make for Him a house in which He could live. He told Moses how it was to be made.

Because the children of Israel were traveling, God's house would need to be one that could be moved. So it was a large tent.

Because very many of the people around Israel worshiped idols, the children of Israel would be tempted to do the same thing. God did not want them to be like other people. They were His own special people, and He wanted them to do better things than the people around them. He wanted them to love and worship Him even though they could not see Him. He thought it best to give them a place in which they could meet with Him. Even though they could not see God, yet they could know He was there.

This tent in which God was to live was very beautiful. God told Moses just how it was to be made. The people gave of their gold and silver to help make the house in which God was to live. This tent was set up in the middle of their camping ground.

They worshiped God in a different way than we do today, because they lived before Jesus came to die so that our sins could be taken away. When they worshiped God, they brought an offering to Him. Often this offering was a lamb. The lamb had to be killed. This was to help them think of Jesus who would sometime die to take away their sins.

When God was through telling Moses how to make the tent in which He would live and how the people should worship Him, He gave Moses two pieces of stone on which were the ten commandments. You would think it would be hard to write on stone, but God wrote the commandments on the stone with His finger.

# The People Sin

Exodus 32:1-20

You remember that Moses was up on the mountain talking with God forty days and forty nights. The children of Israel could not see Moses because a thick cloud covered the mountain. They became tired of waiting for him to come down to them again. They came to Aaron and said, "You make us gods to lead us because we do not know what has become of Moses, the man who brought us out of Egypt."

This was a very wicked thing which the children of Israel asked Aaron to do. The very first of the ten commandments God had given to them said that they were not to have other gods. God wanted them to believe that He was with them and would lead them and take care of them even if they could not see Him.

Aaron should have helped the people to see that what they asked for was not good, but instead he made them gods. He told the people to give him their gold. Then he melted it so that it would be soft and could be shaped into the image of a calf. The people said that these were the gods which had brought them up out of the land of Egypt! The next day the people had a big feast. They ate and drank and played as though they were having a very good time.

God could see what the people were doing while He was talking to Moses, but Moses could not see them. So God told Moses what the people were doing. He said, "Go down, because the people whom you brought out of Egypt have sinned. They have made a calf and are worshiping it. They are saying that these are the gods which brought them out of Egypt."

The Lord was angry with the people for doing such a wicked thing. He was going to destroy them. But Moses asked God not to destroy them, so God did not destroy them.

Then Moses turned and went down the mountain. He took with him the two pieces of stone on which God had written the ten commandments. He met Joshua, his helper.

When Joshua heard the noise the people were making, he thought it sounded as though they were having a war in the camp. But Moses thought it sounded as though the people were singing.

When they came near the camp, Moses saw the calf they had made, and he saw the people dancing around it. When Moses saw the terrible thing they were doing, he became angry. He threw down the two pieces of stone, and they broke into pieces. Then he took the calf they had made and burned it. He ground it into fine pieces and threw it into the water and made the children of Israel drink the water.

## Lesson 26
# The People Are Punished
### Exodus 32:21-34:35

Moses said to Aaron, "What did the people do to you that you brought such a great sin upon them?"

Aaron answered, "Do not be angry. You know how the people are. They told me to make gods to go before them because they did not know what had happened to you. I told them if they had any gold they should give it to me. So they gave me their gold, I put it into the fire, and this calf came out." He did not say that he had made the calf for them.

Then Moses went out and stood in the gate of the camp and said, "Who is on the Lord's side? Let him come to me." Only the tribe of Levi came. Moses told these men to come to him. Then he said to them, "This is what God says, 'You take your swords and go in and out of the gates in the camp and kill the people.' " So these men killed about three thousand men that day.

Moses said to the people who were left, "You have sinned a great sin, but I will go to the Lord to see whether He will forgive your sin."

Moses went to the Lord and said, "Oh, these people have sinned a great sin and have made them gods of gold." Then he asked the Lord to forgive their sin. He told the Lord that if He would not forgive them, he himself was willing to suffer with the people.

But God said that only the people who sinned would suffer. He told Moses to go and lead them on to the land where they were to go. God promised to go with them into the land.

The Lord told Moses to cut out two pieces of stone like the first ones that had been broken. God said that He would write the ten commandments on them. Moses went up on the mountain with God another forty days and nights, and all this time he did not eat any food or drink any water. There God told Moses many things so that Moses could go back and tell the people what God had said.

This time while Moses was gone forty days and nights, the people did not make an idol to worship. They had learned their lesson.

Moses came down from the mountain. He brought along the two pieces of stone and talked to the people. He did not know it, but his face was shining while he was talking to them. When Aaron and the other people looked at Moses and saw his face shining, they were afraid to come near him. Finally Moses had to put a veil over his face because it was so bright that the people could not stand to look at it.

Lesson 27

# The People Leave Sinai

Exodus 40:34-38; Leviticus 8:1-10:7; Numbers 10:11-11:33

God chose the tribe of Levi to take care of the house of God and to look after the offerings. Aaron was the high priest and his sons helped him in the work. The fire that was on the altar was never to go out. God Himself had started this fire, so it was very special.

One day the two older sons of Aaron used another fire in the work of the Lord. God did not like this, and He sent a fire that killed them. After this the two younger sons of Aaron took their place in the work of the Lord.

The people camped near Mount Sinai for nearly a year. But they were busy because it was there that they built the house of God. When this building was finished, the cloud covered it. This was a sign to them that God was there. From the evening until the morning the cloud was a pillar of fire.

This is the way it was throughout their travels. As long as the cloud stayed on the tabernacle, the people rested. When the cloud went up from the tabernacle, they knew God wanted them to travel again. So they would take down the tents and get ready to travel. They never knew how long they would stay in one place. Sometimes it was just two days. Sometimes it was a month and sometimes a year.

Now the time had come that God wanted them to leave the mountain called Sinai. The cloud went up and the people started on their way.

The people started grumbling again. We do not know what they grumbled about, but we do know that God does not want His people to grumble. He sent fire to burn the people. When Moses prayed for the people, the fire was put out.

After this the people started grumbling because they were tired of eating manna. They remembered some of the things that they had to eat in Egypt, and they wished for those things. It made Moses tired to hear them grumble so much. The Lord became angry with the people, too.

Moses said to God, "Why must I take care of all these people?" He also asked, "Where can I find enough meat to feed them? They are asking for meat to eat." He told God that he would rather die than take care of these grumbling people.

The Lord told Moses that He was going to send them meat to eat until they were so full of it that they could not stand to eat it. God punished them for their grumbling.

## Lesson 28

# The Sin of Aaron and Miriam.

### Numbers 12

Even Moses' brother Aaron and his sister Miriam found fault with Moses. They said, "Does the Lord speak to us only by Moses? Hasn't the Lord spoken to us, too?" It seems that they were jealous because God talked to Moses more than He talked to them.

The Lord heard what they said, and He was not pleased. Moses did not think that he was a great man or better than the other people. God had given Moses a hard work to do, and Moses was trying to do the work that God had given him. They should not have been finding fault with him and making his work harder. They should have been trying to help him.

God called to Moses and Aaron and

Miriam and told them to come to the tabernacle. So the three of them went to the tabernacle and the Lord came down in the cloud by the door of the tabernacle to talk to them. He called for Aaron and Miriam to come to Him.

God let them know He had chosen to talk to Moses. He asked them why they were not afraid to say anything against Moses. Then the Lord went away in the cloud. After the cloud went up, Aaron looked at Miriam, and he saw something was wrong. Miriam had a terrible disease called leprosy. Aaron felt very bad that Miriam had to suffer like this when he had sinned, too. He told Moses that they had sinned and asked him to pray to God for them.

Moses prayed to God and asked Him to heal Miriam. Miriam had to stay away from the other people for seven days. Then the Lord let her come back into the camp, and they traveled on again.

When a person had leprosy, he was not allowed to be with other people who did not have the disease. If he would be with other people, the others might get the disease from him. Leprosy was a very bad disease that no one wanted to get.

# Ten Wicked Men and Two Faithful Men

Numbers 13:1-14:4

By this time the children of Israel were coming close to the land to which God was leading them. God told Moses to send men into the land to look it over and see what it was like. Then they were to come back and tell the people what they had found.

Moses sent twelve men into the land. He told them to see whether the people of the land were strong or weak and whether there were many people or only a few. They were to see whether the land was good or bad and find out what kind of houses the people lived in. He told them to be brave and to bring back some of the fruit they found in the land. It was the time of the year when the grapes were beginning to get ripe. If these men went ahead to look over the land, they would know better where and how to take the rest of the people into the land.

These men were gone forty days. When they came back, they brought along some of the good fruit they found there. They found a bunch of grapes so large that two men carried it on a pole between them. They showed this fruit to the people and told them about the land and the people in it. They said that the land was a very good land but the people were taller than they. They said that the people were very strong and that they lived in big cities with high walls around them. Ten of the men who had gone thought they should not try to go into the land. They thought they would be in danger of losing their lives because there were such big people living there.

But two of the men were faithful. Their names were Joshua and Caleb.

Caleb was not afraid. He knew that God would help them fight their enemies. He said, "Let us go up right away, for we are well able to overcome the people."

But the other ten men said, "No, we are not able to go up against these people. They are much stronger than we. We saw giants there and beside them we looked like grasshoppers."

That night the children of Israel cried. They grumbled about Moses and Aaron bringing them into a land where they would be killed by these big giants. They thought it would have been better if they had died in Egypt or even right where they were. They decided to choose someone else to be their leader and go back to the land of Egypt.

## Lesson 30

# More Sin in the Camp

Numbers 14:6-45

Joshua and Caleb felt very bad when they heard that the people did not want to go into the good land that God had promised to give them. They said, "The land that we went into is a very good land. If the Lord wants to be good to us, He will bring us into this land and will give it to us. Do not go against what God wants you to do and do not be afraid of the people of this land. They do not have help as we do. The Lord is with us."

But the people would not listen to Joshua and Caleb. They wanted to kill them.

Then the Lord came. He wanted to destroy all these wicked people. Moses prayed for them and the Lord forgave them. But He had to punish them. He told them that those of them who did not obey could not go into the good land. Only their children would be able to go in. The children of Israel would need to keep traveling around as they had been doing until they all died, and then at the end of forty years their children would go into the land.

But God said that Joshua and Caleb would go in. They were not wicked like all the other people. The other ten men who went up with Joshua and Caleb soon died for bringing back the bad story that made the people afraid to go into the land.

When Moses told the people what their punishment was, they cried again. They said, "We will go into the land the Lord promised to give us. We have sinned in not wanting to go in."

But Moses told them that they should not go because the Lord would not be with them. They would be sinning more if they tried to go in after God told them not to go. The Lord would not fight for them, and they would be killed.

But they would not listen to Moses. They tried to go into the land. But the people of the land came out to fight them, and the people of Israel lost the war.

# Unit ③

## More About Moses
## Balaam
## Israel in Canaan

# Bible Memory Verses

1. Blessed is he whose transgression is forgiven. Psalm 32:1

2. Blessed is the nation whose God is the Lord. Psalm 33:12

3. Blessed is every one that feareth the Lord. Psalm 128:1

4. Blessed are they that hear the word of God, and keep it. Luke 11:28

5. Blessed is the man that maketh the Lord his trust. Psalm 40:4

6. Blessed is the man that walketh not in the counsel of the ungodly. Psalm 1:1

Lesson 1

# A New Thing

Numbers 16:1-35

Among the children of Israel there were wicked men who thought Moses and Aaron tried to make themselves too great. They came to Moses and told him what they thought.

Moses did not feel that he was a great man just because he was the leader of so many people. He was their leader because God wanted him to be their leader. Moses had been a good leader for the people. But the people had often grumbled and made it hard for him. Moses felt very bad when he heard these men find fault with him. He fell down on his face. He told them that tomorrow the Lord would show them who God's people were.

Moses called for some of the men who

found fault to come to him. But they would not come. They were angry with Moses, and they did not want to obey him. They said that Moses had brought them out of Egypt into this wilderness to die. They found fault with him for not taking them into the land of Canaan. This was a very bad thing for them to do. It was not Moses' fault that they did not get to go into the land of Canaan. When the Lord wanted to take them into Canaan, they were afraid and would not go. So it was their own fault that they could not go into the land of Canaan.

Moses was not pleased that these men would not come when he called for them. The Lord showed Moses what he should do. He told him to tell the other people to get away from these wicked men.

Moses said to the people, "Get away from the tents of these wicked men and do not touch anything of theirs, or you will die."

So the people on all sides got away from these men. Then these wicked men and the wives and children of two of these men came and stood in the door of their tents.

Moses said to the people, "This is the way you can know that the Lord sent me to do this work. If these men die the way that most people die, then you can know that the Lord did not send me. But if the Lord does something new and makes the earth open up and swallow these men and everything that they have, then you will know that God is not pleased with what these men have done."

When Moses said this, the ground began to open up under them. All these men and their families went down alive into this big hole in the earth. Even their tents went down with them. Then the earth closed up again and buried them. These people screamed as they went down alive, but no one could help them.

214

The other people were so much afraid that they ran away from the screaming people. Now the people knew that God had sent Moses to be their leader. They knew that these men were wicked to grumble about Moses.

After this the Lord sent a fire to burn up more of the wicked men.

## Lesson 2

# More Sin

Numbers 16:41-17:13 and 20:1

We would think that by this time all the people would be afraid to say bad things about Moses and Aaron. They saw how the Lord punished the people who had talked against them. But the very next day all the people found fault with Moses and Aaron. They said, "You have killed God's people."

We know that it was not Moses and Aaron who killed the people. God had punished the people for their own sin. He had made the earth open up and swallow them. He had sent fire to destroy some of the others.

God was very much displeased with the people for finding fault again. He came down in a cloud and covered the tabernacle. He told Moses to get away from these people because He was going to destroy them. Many, many people died that day. Many, many more people would have died, but Aaron went to God for help so that they all would not need to die.

The Lord did not want the people to find fault with their leaders anymore. He wanted them to know that He had chosen Moses and Aaron for this great work. So He had twelve men bring their rods to Moses. Moses laid them in the tabernacle.

When Moses went into the tabernacle the next day, he found that something had happened to Aaron's rod. It was blooming like a fruit tree would bloom, and it had nuts on it.

Moses brought all the rods out and gave them back to the men to whom they belonged. They could see that God had done something special to Aaron's rod.

That meant God had called Aaron to this special work. God told Moses to take Aaron's rod back into the tabernacle again. It was to stay there to remind the people that God had chosen Aaron.

After this, the time came that Miriam, the older sister of Moses and Aaron, must die. So she died and was buried there in the wilderness.

## Lesson 3

# Water and Snakes

Numbers 20:2-21:9

While the children of Israel were still at the place where Miriam died, they could not find any water to drink. So what do you suppose they did? They did what they had done so often before. They grumbled. They found fault with Moses for bringing them out into the wilderness to die.

Moses and Aaron went to the door of the tabernacle and fell on their faces. There the Lord talked to Moses. He said, "Take the rod and bring the people together. Speak to the rock while all the people are watching. Then the rock will give you water to drink. This is the way you can give water to the people and to their animals."

So Moses took the rod as God had told him to do. Then he and Aaron gathered the people together. But Moses did not speak to the rock as God had told him to do. He was angry with the people because they had grumbled. In his anger he hit the rock instead of speaking to it. Even though Moses did not obey, God gave the people water out of the rock. Moses hit the rock twice and water came out. There was water for the people and the animals to drink.

But because Moses did not obey God, God said He would punish him. God told him that he could not go into the good land that He was going to give to the children of Israel. This was a hard punishment for Moses. For nearly forty years he had hoped someday to get to this good land and now he would never get to go into the land.

After this the children of Israel traveled on to another place. They came to a mountain. Here God told Moses that his brother Aaron must die. He told him to take Aaron and his son up to the mountain. While all the other people were watching, Moses and Aaron and his son went up on the mountain. There on the mountain, Aaron died. God told Moses to make Aaron's son the high priest instead of his father.

Then the children of Israel traveled on to another place. But they grumbled against God and Moses again. They grumbled for bread to eat. God was feeding them manna, but they were tired of it. They had been eating manna for nearly forty years.

God was displeased with them for grumbling. He sent snakes that bit the people and made them die. Many of the people died. The other people were probably afraid they would die, too. So they came to Moses and said, "We have sinned. Pray to the Lord that He will take away the snakes." So Moses prayed for the people.

God said to Moses, "Make a snake out of brass. Hang it up on a pole. Then when anyone is bitten by a snake, if he looks at the snake on the pole, he will live."

So Moses made a snake out of brass and hung it on a pole. Then if the people were bitten by a snake, they would not need to die. If they looked at the snake on the pole, they would live. Of course, if they would not look, they would die.

Lesson 4

# Balaam Called

Numbers 22:1-21

By this time the children of Israel were very close to the land to which God was taking them. The people who lived there saw the children of Israel in their land. They were very much afraid of Israel because there were so many of them. So the king of this land sent men to a man called Balaam who lived not far away. He wanted Balaam to come and curse the children of Israel.

The king's men came to Balaam and said, "There is a group of people who came out of the land of Egypt, and they cover the earth. Now they are living close to me. Please come and curse them so that we can kill them and drive them out of the land. I know that whoever you curse is cursed, and whoever you bless is blessed."

Balaam said, "You stay here tonight, and I will tell you what God says to me." So the men stayed there with Balaam that night.

God came to Balaam that night and asked, "What men are here with you?" Balaam told God who they were and why they had come. God said, "Do not go with them. You are not supposed to curse these people because they are blessed."

The next morning Balaam said to the men, "Go back to your land. The Lord will not let me go with you."

So the men went back to the king without Balaam. They told the king that Balaam would not come along.

But the king wanted Balaam to come. He was afraid of the children of Israel, and he wanted Balaam to come and curse them. If they were cursed, God would not help them, and then maybe he could fight them and drive them out. But he was afraid to fight them if their God was helping them. He had probably heard about the great things God had already done for them. So the king sent more men to Balaam to try again to get him to come. They came to Balaam and said, "The king says not to let anything stop you from coming to him. If you will come and curse Israel, he will make you a great man. He will do for you anything that you want him to do."

This sounded good to Balaam and he wanted very much to go. God had already told him he should not go. He did not want to obey. So he asked God again. It was wrong for him to do this because God had already told him not to go.

But Balaam went anyway. The next morning Balaam got up and got his donkey ready to ride. He went along with the men to go to the king. Two of Balaam's servants went along with him.

Lesson 5

# The Donkey Talks

Numbers 22:22-24:25

The Lord was not pleased that Balaam went, so He sent His angel to stand in the path on which they were traveling. The angel had a sword in his hand. The Lord kept Balaam from seeing him. But the donkey saw the angel standing in the path. So she went off the path into the field. Balaam did not know what made the donkey go off the path into the field, and he did not like it. He hit the donkey to try to make her go back onto the path again.

The angel went and stood in a place where there was a wall on both sides of the path. When the donkey saw the angel in the way, she went over against the wall to try to get out of the angel's way.

When she threw herself against the wall, it crushed Balaam's foot. Balaam did not know what was wrong with his donkey, but he did not like the way she was acting. So he hit her again. Then the angel went further and stood in a very narrow place where the donkey could not turn to get out of the path. When the donkey saw the angel, she fell down to the ground. Now Balaam was very angry and took a stick and hit the donkey.

Then what do you suppose happened? God made the donkey talk. Can you imagine a donkey talking to a man? This one did. She said to Balaam, "What have I done to you that you have hit me these three times?"

Balaam was so angry at the donkey that he said, "I wish I had a sword in my hand. Then I would kill you."

The donkey said, "Am I not your donkey that you have ridden ever since I belonged to you? Did I ever do this way to you?"

Balaam answered, "No." Then the Lord let Balaam see the angel, too. He saw him standing in the path with the sword in his hand. Balaam bowed his head and fell flat on his face.

The angel said to Balaam, "Why did you hit your donkey these three times? I came to try to keep you from going because it is wrong for you to go with these men. The donkey saw me and got out of my way these three times. If she had not done that, I would have killed you and saved the donkey."

Balaam said, "I have sinned. Now if you do not want me to go, I will go back home again."

The angel told him he could go, but he should say only the things that he told him to say. So Balaam went on with the men.

When he came to the king, he told the king that he would have to say only what

God told him to say. So Balaam had to
speak only what God let him speak. God
would not let him curse Israel. He had
Balaam bless Israel instead. When the
king heard Balaam bless Israel, it made
him angry. He told Balaam to run back
home. He told Balaam that he had planned
to make him a great man but now he
would not. So Balaam went back home
again.

# Moses Sees the Promised Land

Deuteronomy 3:23-34:7

The children of Israel had been in the wilderness a long time. It was nearly forty years since they had left Egypt. All this time God had taken very good care of them. Their clothes did not wear out in all this time.

By this time, most of the men who had been wicked and disobeyed God had died. Soon God was going to let their children go into the good land that He had said He would give to them. But even Moses did not get to go into the land. He, too, had disobeyed God when he hit the rock instead of speaking to it. Moses wanted very much to go into the land. He asked God to please let him go into the land. But God told him that he could not go into the land. He told him he should not ask to go in anymore. God told him to go up to the top of a mountain. There he could see the good land that God was going to give them. So Moses was able to see the land even though he could not go into it.

Because Moses could not go into the land, the people would need a new leader to lead them into this good land. God chose Joshua, a man who obeyed Him, to be this new leader.

Before Moses died he told the children of Israel many things. He told them what they should do when they got into the good land. He told them if they would obey God, God would be with them and help them. But if they would not obey God, God would make it hard for them. God wanted them to destroy the wicked people who were living in that land.

The time came that Moses must die. God told him to go up to the top of the mountain. God showed him the good land of Canaan. There on the mountain, Moses died. God took him to a valley to bury him. Nobody knows where Moses' grave is. God buried him. When Moses died he was one hundred twenty years old. But he was different from the way many old men are before they die. Many are weak and cannot see or hear very well. Moses was still a strong man, and he could still see very well.

# The People Get Ready to Go Into the Good Land

Joshua 1:1-2:7

After Moses was dead, God talked to Joshua, the new leader. He said, "Moses is dead. Get up and go over the Jordan River. You and all the people shall go over into this land that I will give to them. Every place you walk, that land will be yours."

Joshua sent men to the people to tell them to get food ready. Within three days they were to go over the Jordan River into the good land of Canaan.

Joshua told the people what to do, and the people said to Joshua, "All that you tell us to do, we will do. Wherever you send us, we will go. Anyone who does not do as you tell him to do shall be put to death." These words of the people were good words. Now would they really do as they said they would do?

Joshua sent two men into the new land to look it over. He wanted them to try not to let the people of the land see them. These two men went to the city of Jericho. There they stayed at the house of a woman called Rahab.

We do not know how, but someone found out that these two men were there. They came to the king and said, "Men of Israel have come in the night to look at our country."

The king told Rahab to bring the men who had come to her house. But Rahab wanted to help these men. She did not bring them to the king. She hid them instead. Then she said to the king, "Two men came, but I did not know where they were from. When it got dark, these men went away. I did not know where they went. Hurry and go after them. You can catch up with them."

The king sent men out to try to find them, but all this time they were hidden by stalks of flax which Rahab had laid out on the top of her house.

The men hurried to try to catch up with the men of Israel, but, of course, they could not find them.

Lesson 8

# Rahab's Kindness

Joshua 2:8-24

While the men were gone, Rahab went up to where she had hid the men. She said to them, "I know that the Lord has given you this land. All the people here in this land are afraid of you. We have heard how the Lord dried up the Red Sea for you, when you came up out of Egypt. We heard about the kings that you destroyed. When we heard this, we were very much afraid because of you, because your God is in heaven and on the earth. Now please promise me that because I have been kind to you, you will be kind to me and my family. Do not kill my father or mother or brothers or sisters."

The two men answered, "If you will not tell anyone about us and why we came here, we will be kind to you."

The city of Jericho had a high, thick wall around it. Rahab's house was on this wall. She let the two men down over the wall with a rope. Then they could get away without anyone in the city seeing them. She told them to go to the mountains and hide three days until the men who went to look for them would get back. Then it would be safe for them to go home.

The men said to her, "Take this red rope that you used to let us down, and put it in the window. Then all of your family shall stay in the house. If you keep quiet about our business and all stay in the house and have this red rope in the window, then you will be saved. But if you do not do these things, we will not save you when we come into the land."

Rahab said she would do as they told her to do. She sent them away and put the red rope in the window. The men stayed in the mountains until the men who were looking for them came back again. Then they went back over the Jordan River and told Joshua about all the things that had happened to them. They said, "It is true that God will give us this land because all the people are afraid of us."

# Going Over Jordan

Joshua 3:1-5:15

Joshua got up early the next morning. He and the people came to the Jordan River. There Joshua told the people what they should do. He told the priests to go over the Jordan first and carry with them the ark from the tabernacle. He told the people to follow the priests.

As the priests' feet stepped into the edge of the water of the Jordan River, the waters parted and stood up so that the people could go over on dry ground. The priests stood in the middle of the Jordan with the ark of God until all the people came to the other side of the Jordan River.

Now for the first time they were in the land that God had promised to give them.

The place where they came over was very close to the city of Jericho. Here by the river they set up twelve stones. When their children would ask their fathers what these stones meant, they were to tell them what the Lord had done for them at the Jordan River. As soon as everyone was on the other side of the river, the waters came back again into their place.

The people in this land heard how God had dried up the waters of the Jordan River so that the people could come over. They were very much afraid when they heard this. They knew that these people had a very great God. The gods they worshiped, which were idols, could not do anything for them.

God did not send the children of Israel manna very long after they were in this good land. They could eat the good fruit they found in the land of Canaan.

When Joshua was near Jericho, he

looked up and saw near him a man with a sword in his hand. Joshua went over to him. He asked him whether he had come to help them fight, or whether he was their enemy. The man said he was a captain from God. Then Joshua fell down to the ground and asked him what he had to say. God's captain said, "Take your shoe off your foot, because the land that you are standing on is holy ground." Joshua took off his shoe.

Do you remember the time God told Moses to take off his shoes? Now He asked Joshua to take off his shoe. God wanted Joshua to know that He would be with him as He had been with Moses.

# How Jericho Was Destroyed
### Joshua 6:1-7:1

The first city that God wanted the children of Israel to destroy was Jericho. The people of Jericho were so afraid that none of them came outside the big walls of their city. They all stayed inside.

God told Joshua what they were to do, and Joshua told the people what God said. Joshua said, "All the men of war shall go around the city one time each day for six days. On the seventh day they shall go around the city seven times. The seven priests that go before the ark shall take with them seven trumpets. While they walk around the city the priests shall blow their trumpets. But the people are not to make any noise with their voices. They are not to say even one

word until I tell them to shout. Then all of them are supposed to shout."

The people did as they were told to do. The first day they marched around the city once. The second day they marched around the city again. They did this every day for six days. On the seventh day they got up very early in the morning, just about the time it was starting to get light. They marched around the city seven times. After they had gone around the seventh time, Joshua said to the people, "Shout." All the people shouted and the walls of the city fell down flat. Now it was easy to get to the people of Jericho. They went into the city and killed all the people and the animals.

But Rahab and all her family were saved because she had done everything the men told her to do. After that, Rahab and her family lived with the children of Israel.

We can see that God helped the

children of Israel in wonderful ways when they obeyed Him. The other people in the land of Canaan also heard how God helped the children of Israel.

Before they destroyed Jericho, God had told them they could take the gold and silver that they found in this city and give it to the Lord, but they were not to keep any of it for themselves. There was one man who disobeyed. When he saw the gold and silver, he wanted to keep some for himself. He took some and hid it in his tent. Joshua did not know that he had taken any gold or silver, but God knew it.

## Lesson 11
# Why Israel Lost a Battle
Joshua 7:2-26

After the children of Israel had destroyed Jericho, Joshua sent men to another city. He wanted them to look at it to see what kind of city it was. The name of this city was Ai. After the men had gone and looked at the city, they came back again to Joshua. They said, "There are not many people in this city. Not all the men will need to go to fight against it."

Only about three thousand men were sent to fight against the people of Ai. But God did not help Israel, and Israel did not win the battle. The men of Ai chased them away. This made the people of Israel very much afraid. Here they were in a new land, and there were many enemies. Why did God not help them as He had said He would? They did not know.

When Joshua heard that Israel had lost the battle, he tore his clothes and fell down to the ground. Joshua asked God, "Why have You brought these people over the Jordan River to destroy them? When the other people hear about this, they will destroy us, and what will it do to Your great Name?"

God told Joshua to get up. It was not that God could not help them. It was because they had sinned. Someone had taken from Jericho something that he was not supposed to take, and God would not help them until they got rid of it.

They had to find out who had done this wicked thing. At last God showed them who it was. His name was Achan.

Joshua said to Achan, "My son, please tell me what you have done. Do not hide it from me."

Achan said, "I have sinned. When I saw the gold and silver, I wanted them and took them. They are hid in my tent."

Joshua sent men to Achan's tent to find the things. They found all the things that Achan had stolen and brought them to Joshua.

Joshua and all Israel took Achan, his family, his animals, the things he had stolen, and everything he had to a valley. Joshua said to Achan, "Why did you trouble us? The Lord will trouble you today." All the people stoned him with stones. After that, they burned his things with fire.

Now the Lord was not angry with the people. He could help them win their battles.

# God Helps Israel Fight Ai

Joshua 8

The Lord said to Joshua, "Do not be afraid. Take all the men of war with you and go up to the city of Ai and take it. Destroy all the people as you have done with the people of Jericho. Only this time you may keep animals and other things for yourselves."

Joshua divided the men into two groups. He sent one group to hide behind the city. The other group was to go with him. To the first group he said, "Go and hide behind the city, but not very far away from the city. Then I and the people who are with me will go up to the city. When the people in the city see us, they will come out to fight against us. We will start running away as though we are

afraid of them. They will think they are
winning the battle as they did the first
time. While they are chasing us, you
men who are hiding behind the city can
come into the city and take their things.
God will give it to you. You are supposed
to set the city on fire."

These men went and hid behind the
city. The king of Ai did not know that
they were there. The next day Joshua
and his men went up to the city of Ai.
When the king of Ai saw them, he hurried
and got his men ready to go out and fight
with them. The king and all his men went
out of the city and left the gates open.
There was not one man left in Ai. They
all went out to fight against Israel.

The men with Joshua pretended they
were afraid and started running away
from their enemies. Of course, their
enemies followed after them. God said
to Joshua, "Hold up your spear toward
Ai." So Joshua held up his spear. When

the men who were hiding behind the city saw Joshua hold up his spear, they got up quickly and went into the city and set it on fire.

The men of Ai looked behind them. They saw that their city was on fire. Now their homes were gone. They had enemies in front of them and behind them. They had no place to go to get away from them. The people of Israel stopped running away from them and turned around and killed them.

Joshua thanked the Lord for what He had done for them. Also he read to the people the things that Moses had written to remind the children of Israel what they were to do and what they were not to do.

## Lesson 13
# Tricky People Trick Israel
### Joshua 9:3-27

In the land of Canaan there was a town called Gibeon. The people in this town heard what Israel had done to Jericho and Ai. They were very much afraid of Israel. They thought of a plan to trick them. They sent to Joshua some men who pretended they had come from a very far country to bring him a message. They put very old sacks on their animals. They took bottles made of skins that were old and cracked, but patched. They put very old shoes on their feet and put on old clothes. They took with them bread that was dry and moldy. Then they went to Joshua. They said, "We come from a far country. Now let us join you."

The men of Israel said, "What if you

live here in this land?" They knew that they were supposed to kill the people in this land. They said, "How shall we join with you?"

The men of Gibeon said, "We will be your servants."

Joshua said, "Who are you and from where did you come?"

They answered, "We have come from a very far country because we heard about your God. We heard about the things He did in Egypt. We were sent to you to tell you that we will be your servants. Now let us join you. We took this bread when it was hot, but now you can see that it is dry and moldy. These bottles were new, but now they are torn. Our clothes and shoes have become old because we have been on such a long journey."

The men of Israel could see that the food was old, but they did not ask the Lord what they should do. Joshua believed what they said. He promised that he would never kill them.

Three days later, the children of Israel heard that these people were living close to them in the land of Canaan. They went over to their town to see them, but they did not kill them because they had promised that they would not. It would not be right for them to break their promise. They should have been more careful before they made such a promise. They did not kill them, but they made them to be their servants. The men of Gibeon had to split wood and carry water for the children of Israel.

Lesson 14

# Israel Helps Gibeon

Joshua 10:1-11:23

One of the kings in the land heard that the Gibeonites had joined themselves to Israel. He had also heard how the children of Israel had destroyed Jericho and her king and Ai and her king. He was very much afraid because now Israel had the Gibeonites to help them fight their enemies. So this king called four other kings to come and help him fight against Gibeon.

When the Gibeonites knew about this, they sent word to Joshua to come and help them fight. Joshua and his mighty men started out to help the men of Gibeon. The Lord told Joshua not to be afraid to help the Gibeonites fight because He would help them destroy their enemies. As they fought with them, their enemies tried to run away from them. The Lord threw great hailstones out of heaven upon them. More people were killed by the hailstones than by the swords of Joshua and his men.

Joshua asked God to let the sun and the moon stand still so that they could finish fighting. So the sun did not go down about a whole day. There was never a day like that before, and there has never been a day like that since.

Joshua and his men came back to camp. The five kings ran away and hid themselves in a cave. Someone came and told Joshua that the five kings had hidden themselves in a cave. Joshua told them to put big stones at the mouth of the cave and let men there by the cave to watch it. Then they went and finished fighting their enemies. When they finished, Joshua told them to bring the five kings out of the cave. Joshua killed them and buried them in the cave where they had hidden themselves.

Many, many cities were destroyed at this time because the Lord helped the children of Israel. They killed all the people who lived in these cities.

There were still many, many more cities that needed to be taken. God helped them, and for a time the fighting was over. The people settled down to live in this new land that God had given to them.

God did every good thing which He had said He would do for them.

## Lesson 15
# Living in the New Land
### Joshua 13:7-22:34

The people of Israel settled in their new land according to their tribes. You remember that Jacob had twelve sons. And you remember that Jacob's name had been changed to Israel. Each of these sons was the leader of a tribe in Israel. Joseph had two sons. Each son was the leader of a tribe and got a separate part of the land. The land was divided according to the tribes.

Every tribe got a certain amount of land except the tribe of Levi. The Levites were not to own any land. They were not to raise many crops. They were not to help fight when there was any fighting to be done. Their work was a special part of the Lord's work. They were to take care of the tabernacle. The other tribes were to give them places to live and see to it that they had what they needed. The Levites were to get some of their living from the land they got from the other tribes.

The enemies that remained in the land where these tribes settled were to be driven out. If a tribe needed help, they could ask another tribe to help them.

God told the people to build cities of refuge in this land. If anyone happened to kill another person, but did not mean to kill him, he could run to this city. As long as he stayed in this city, he would be safe. If he did not stay in the city, he could be killed. He must stay in the city until the high priest died if he wanted to be safe.

When Joshua was old, he called together the older men and the leaders of Israel. He told them to have great courage. He told them to be sure to do what

God told them to do. He told them that if they obeyed God, God would fight for them. But he also told them that if they would not obey, life in this new land would be hard for them.

## Lesson 16

# After the Death of Joshua

Joshua 23:1-Judges 2:23

The time came when Joshua was an old man. He died when he was one hundred ten years old. All the time that Joshua lived, the people of Israel obeyed God and did what was right. Even awhile after Joshua died they obeyed God. There still were old men living to tell them the wonderful things that God had done for them.

Do you remember what the children of Israel carried with them all the time they were in the wilderness? They carried the bones of Joseph for forty years because Joseph wanted to be buried in the land of Canaan. Now that they were finally settled in the land of Canaan, they buried Joseph's bones.

After this some of the people of Israel went out to fight against the people of Canaan. God helped them to win the battle. There was one man who ran away from them. They ran after him and caught him. They cut off his thumbs and his big toes. This was not a very nice way to be treated, but the man knew he deserved to be treated this way. He said, "Seventy kings, who had their thumbs and big toes cut off, ate at my table. As I have done to them, God has done to me." The men of Israel brought this man to Jerusalem, and he died there.

Then a sad thing happened. The children of Israel did not destroy all their enemies as God wanted them to do. They let them live with them. Then they did not follow God and worship Him. They began to worship the gods and idols of the people around them. God could not help them as He had said He would if they would obey Him. He let their enemies make life hard for them. When they cried to the Lord for help, the Lord helped them. Soon they would be back in sin again. This happened over and over again. God listened to them when they were in trouble and helped them. They did not deserve it, but God was very good to them.

## Lesson 17

# Ehud Helps Israel

Judges 3:12-30

One time after the children of Israel had sinned, God made the king of Moab strong. He was one of their enemies. He fought with Israel and made the people of Israel his servants. They were his servants for eighteen years. Then they asked the Lord to help them. The Lord got a man ready to help them. His name was Ehud. He was a left-handed man.

The children of Israel sent Ehud with a present to the king who was making life hard for them. The king's name was Eglon, and he was a very fat man. Ehud went with a dagger hidden in his clothes so that the king would not know he had a dagger with him.

Ehud went in to the king with the

present he had brought and gave it to the king. Then he told the king he had a secret to tell him. The king told all his men to go out of the room so that Ehud could tell him the secret while they were alone.

When all the other men had gone out of the room, Ehud got up out of his seat and went over to the king. He said, "I have a message from God for you." Then Ehud took out his dagger and stuck it into the belly of the king. The fat closed in around the dagger so that Ehud could not get his dagger out again.

Ehud went out and locked the doors behind him. When the king's servants tried to open the doors, they found they were locked. They thought the king must have locked them. They waited and waited for the king to unlock the doors. Finally, when the king still did not unlock the doors after so long, they took a key and unlocked them. Then they saw that the king was dead.

While the men were waiting to get in to the king, Ehud had gone far away. He went back to the children of Israel and told them to follow him because God was going to help them. Then they could live in peace for a long time again.

Lesson 18

# How a Woman Helped

Judges 4

After Ehud was dead, the children of Israel went back into sin. God let them be servants to another king who made life very hard for them. At last they cried to the Lord for help. They could not help themselves, because this king had nine hundred chariots of iron.

The Lord showed one of the women in Israel what the people should do. He showed her that Israel should go with ten thousand men up to a mountain to fight against the king and his people. God said He would help them.

She called for one of the men of Israel and told him to get ten thousand men and go. This man's name was Barak. Barak said, "If you will go with me, I will go,

267

but if you will not go with me, then I will not go." She said she would go with him.

Barak called the people together and went up to the mountain to fight. Someone told the captain of the king's army that Israel was on the mountain ready to fight with them. The captain got ready his nine hundred chariots of iron and went out to fight against Israel. The Lord helped the people of Israel so that they were able to kill their enemies.

Finally the captain got down out of his chariot and ran away from them. He went to the tent of the people who had told him Israel was going to fight with him and his people. When the woman who lived in the tent saw the captain, she went to meet him. Her name was Jael. She told him not to be afraid, but to come into the tent. There she covered him.

The captain said, "Please give me a little water to drink. I am thirsty." Jael treated him very nicely. Instead of water, she gave him milk to drink. Then she covered him again.

Again the captain talked to Jael. He said, "Stand in the door of the tent. If anyone comes and asks whether there is any man here, tell him there is not."

After a while the captain went to sleep. Jael took a hammer and nail and went in very quietly to where the captain was sleeping. The captain was very tired and was fast asleep. Jael took the nail and pounded it into his head and he died.

Barak was still running after the captain and trying to find him. When Jael saw him coming, she ran out to meet him and said, "Come, I will show you the man for whom you are looking." She took him into the tent and showed him the captain. There he was lying dead.

Once again the Lord helped the children of Israel. They got along well for forty years.

# An Angel Speaks to Gideon

Judges 6:1-24

After forty years the children of Israel began worshiping idols again. The Lord punished them by letting a wicked nation rule over them. The children of Israel made themselves caves and dens to live in to try to hide from their mean enemies. The enemies were called Midianites. If the children of Israel would plant a crop, the Midianites would come and destroy the crop. They took their cattle and sheep away from them. The children of Israel became very poor.

At last they cried to the Lord to help them. The Lord sent a man to them to tell them they had not obeyed Him. He had helped them many times but they did not obey Him.

A man of Israel was thrashing wheat and trying to hide it from the Midianites. While he was there, an angel came to him and said, "The Lord is with you, you mighty man."

This man's name was Gideon. Gideon said to the angel, "Oh my Lord, if the Lord is with us, why has all this happened to us? Where are the things our fathers told us about? Now the Lord is not with us, and He lets all these bad things happen to us."

The angel looked at him and said, "Go, and you will save Israel. Have not I sent you?"

Gideon did not think he could do such a big job and save Israel. But the Lord said that He would be with him and help him save Israel from the Midianites.

Gideon asked the angel to show him for sure that God would do this. He said, "Please do not go away until I come and bring you a present."

The angel of the Lord said, "I will stay until you come again."

Gideon went and got a meal ready for him. He fixed meat and broth and cakes and brought them to him in a basket.

The angel said, "Take the meat and cakes and lay them on this rock and pour out the broth." Gideon did so.

The angel took a staff and touched the meat and the cakes. Fire came up out of the rock and burned them up. Then the angel was gone. Gideon could not see him anymore.

Now Gideon knew this man had been an angel, and he was very much afraid. But God told him not to be afraid.

Lesson 20

# Gideon Destroys Idols

Judges 6:25-40

The same night that the angel came and talked to Gideon, the Lord came and talked to Gideon. He said, "Take your father's young ox and go throw down the altar of Baal that your father has. Cut down the grove that is by it. Then build an altar to the Lord and offer the ox on this altar."

Baal was an idol. God did not want the people to have altars to worship Baal. That is why He wanted Gideon to throw down the altar of Baal and build an altar for Him.

Gideon took ten men to help him. They did it at night because they were afraid to do it in the daytime when others could see them. They threw down the altar of

Baal and cut down the grove. Then they set up an altar to the true God and offered the ox on this altar.

Early the next morning men from the city saw that the altar to Baal had been broken down. They saw that the grove had been cut down, too. They said to each other, "Who has done this thing?" Finally they found out that Gideon had done it.

The men of the city said to Gideon's father, "Bring out your son that he may die, because he has thrown down the altar of Baal and cut down the grove by the altar."

His father said, "If Baal is a god, he can ask for himself." Of course, Baal was just an idol; so he could not ask to have Gideon killed, and nothing was done to Gideon.

The Midianites came to fight against Israel. Gideon called the people to come to him. Gideon wanted to be very sure

God was going to help him. He said to God, "See, I will put a fleece of wool on the floor. If there is dew only on the fleece but not on the ground around it, I will know that You will help me save Israel."

Early the next morning Gideon got up and went to look at the fleece. Sure enough, the fleece was wet with dew. He got a whole bowl full of water out of it. But the ground around the fleece was dry.

Gideon was not quite satisfied. He wanted to make sure once more. So he said, "This time let the fleece of wool be dry but let all the ground around it be wet."

God did that for Gideon. The next morning the fleece was dry, and the ground around the fleece was wet with dew.

Lesson 21

# A Strange Dream

Judges 7:1-15

Gideon and all the people who were with him got up early and got ready to fight the Midianites.

The Lord said to Gideon, "There are too many people here with you. I do not want you to fight with so many people. If so many people fight, they might think they are the ones who won, instead of knowing that I helped them. Go and tell them whoever is afraid should leave."

When Gideon told this to the people, twenty-two thousand left and only ten thousand stayed there.

God said to Gideon, "There are still too many people with you." The Lord told Gideon to take the people down to the water to get a drink. Three hundred of these men drank by putting their hand up to their mouth and lapping the water as a dog would drink. All the other people bowed down on their knees to drink water.

Then God said, "By the three hundred men who lapped I will save you. Let all the other men go back home."

Three hundred men were not very many to go and fight all the Midianites. The Midianite people and those who helped them fight were very, very many, and they had so many animals that they could not be counted. God wanted to show His people He was able to do great things for them.

The people took food in their hands with them, and also their trumpets, to get ready to go. That night the Lord came to Gideon and said, "Get up and go, because I have given your enemies to you. But if you are afraid to go, you and your servant can go down to the enemy's camp. After you hear what they say down there, you will not be afraid to fight them."

Gideon and his servant went down close enough to hear what they said. Gideon heard one man tell another man what he had dreamed. He said, "I dreamed and in my dream I saw a cake of barley bread roll down into our camp. It came to a tent and the tent fell over."

It seemed strange that a little bun would knock a tent over. The man to whom the dream was told knew what this dream meant. He said, "This is nothing else but the sword of Gideon, a man of Israel."

Even though there were only three hundred men in Gideon's army, yet God was going to destroy the big army of the Midianites.

When Gideon heard this dream and what it meant, he thanked God. He felt better because now he knew that God would help them, even though there were not many men with him. Gideon went back to his group of three hundred men and said, "Get up, because God is going to help us."

## Lesson 22
# God Helps Israel
Judges 7:16-8:21

Gideon divided his men into three groups. He put one hundred men in each group. To each man he gave a trumpet and a pitcher with a lamp inside the pitcher. He said to the men, "Look at me and do what I do. When I come to the outside of the camp, you are to do as I do. When I blow my trumpet, you blow your trumpets, too. Then say, 'The sword of the Lord and of Gideon.' "

They went down around the camp of the enemy and blew their trumpets and broke the pitchers that were in their hands. They cried out, "The sword of the Lord and of Gideon."

This scared the Midianites so badly that they screamed and ran away. They even started to kill one another. The men of Israel chased after them. Gideon sent men to tell the men of the tribe of Ephraim to come and help them. They came and were able to kill two of the great men of their enemies. They were not pleased that Gideon had not called for them to come and help sooner. They scolded him very much. Gideon told them that what they did was even greater than what he did because they had killed two great men. Then they felt better and were not angry with Gideon anymore.

There were still two kings which Gideon and his men were going after, and they hoped to kill them. The men who were with him were tired and hungry. He asked some men along the way for some bread to give his men to eat. But they would not give him anything to eat. Gideon told them that after God gave him the two kings, he would tear their flesh with the thorns of the wilderness. He went to another place and asked for something to eat, but they would not give him anything, either. There was a tower at this place. Gideon told them that when he came back he would break down their tower because they would not give him or his men anything to eat.

The kings that Gideon and his men were going after had fifteen thousand men with them. That was all that was left of their army. One hundred twenty thousand had been killed. God gave these two kings to Gideon and made the other men afraid of him. Then the battle was over and Gideon started back before the sun was up. He went back to the places where he had asked for something to eat. At the first place he beat the men with thorns. At the other place he broke down the tower and killed the men of that city.

The two kings that Gideon went after had killed his brothers, so he killed the two kings. He told his oldest son to kill them, but he was afraid to do it because he was still a boy. So Gideon killed them.

Lesson 23
# Abimelech and Jephthah
Judges 8:33-11:40

Again the children of Israel forgot God
and what He had done for them. They
were not kind to Gideon's family. Gideon
had done very much for them.

Gideon had seventy children. One of
his sons, Abimelech, wanted to be the
ruler of the people. He killed all his
brothers except the youngest one. He
could not find his youngest brother because he had hidden himself so that his
brother could not kill him.

Some men got together and made
Abimelech king. But God did not like
what Abimelech had done to his brothers.
One time Abimelech came to a city to
fight against it. There was a strong
tower in this city. Many of the men and

women in the city had gone up into the top of the tower and shut the tower. Abimelech came to this tower and was going to set it on fire. But a woman in the tower had a big stone in her hand. She took it and threw it down on Abimelech. It hurt Abimelech so badly that he thought he was going to die, but he did not want anyone to say that a woman had killed him. He told a young man who was with him to kill him. The young man killed Abimelech. This is the way God punished Abimelech for the wicked things he had done.

After this there was a man whose name was Jephthah. God was with him to help him fight for Israel. Jephthah promised the Lord that if He would help him win the battle, then whatever came to him first when he got home, he would give it to the Lord for a burnt offering. The Lord did help him, and he won the battle.

When he got back home, his daughter came out to meet him. She seemed so happy to see her father again. But her poor father was very sad. This was his only child. He had no other children. And he loved her. He told her what he had promised the Lord.

She said to her father, "If you promised the Lord, you must not go back on your promise." So Jephthah did to her as he had promised the Lord he would do.

## Lesson 24

# A Son Promised

### Judges 13:1-20

Just as they had done so many times before, the children of Israel sinned again. For forty years the Lord made them serve a nation called the Philistines.

One day the angel of God came to a woman in Israel. He said, "You have not had any children. But you will have a son. Be careful that you do not drink any strong drink or eat anything that you should not eat. And never let your son's hair be cut. He will start to help Israel so that they will not need to serve the Philistines."

This woman came to her husband and said, "A man of God came to me. He looked like an angel of God. But I did not ask him where he was from or what his

288

name was. He told me that I am going to
have a son. He told me not to drink any
strong drink or eat anything I should not
eat."

Her husband said to the Lord, "Oh my
Lord, let the man of God whom you sent
come to us and teach us what we shall do
to the child that shall be born."

God heard what the man said. He sent
the angel of God to the woman again while
she was sitting in the field. Her husband
was not there with her. She quickly ran
to her husband to tell him. She said,
"The man who came to me the other day
has come again." Her husband got up and
followed his wife. He came to the angel
and said, "Are you the man who talked to
the woman?"

The angel answered, "I am."

He said, "What shall we do to the
child?"

The angel said to him, "Let the woman
be careful to do everything I told her to

do. She is not to drink any strong drink or eat anything that she should not eat. All that I told her to do, let her do."

The husband said, "Please stay until we get a kid ready for you."

The angel answered, "Even though I stay, I will not eat your bread. And if you offer an offering, you must offer it to the Lord.

The husband said, "What is your name?"

The angel said, "Why do you ask me what my name is, since it is a secret?"

The man and his wife offered the kid as an offering to the Lord, and the angel did some wonderful things while the man and his wife were watching. When the fire went up toward heaven, the angel went up to heaven in the flame. The man and his wife fell to the ground. They were very much afraid.

# Samson, a Strong Man

## Judges 13:21-14:9

The angel did not come to the man and his wife anymore. They knew that the man who had come to them was an angel from God. The man was afraid to think that an angel of God had talked to them. He thought they would die. His wife said, "If the Lord would have wanted to kill us, He would not have taken our offering, or showed us all these things, or told us the things He did."

God did as the angel had told the woman He would do. He gave her a son, and they called him Samson. The boy grew and God helped him.

One day as Samson was gone from home he saw one of the Philistine women. He wanted her to be his wife. He came back to his father and mother and said, "I have seen one of the Philistine women. Get her for me to be my wife."

But his father and mother did not want him to marry a Philistine woman. The Philistines were their enemies. They did not serve the true God. They wanted Samson to find one of the women of Israel to be his wife.

Samson still wanted the Philistine woman. He said, "Get her for me because I like her."

Samson and his father and mother started out to go to where the woman was. On the way, a young lion came out and roared at Samson. God helped Samson. Samson took hold of the lion and tore it to pieces as if it had been a kid instead of a lion. He did not have anything in his hand with which to kill it.

His father and mother were not with him when this happened. They did not see him kill the lion, and Samson did not tell them what he had done.

Samson went on and talked to the woman whom he wanted to be his wife. He liked her very much. After a while he went down to see her again. On the way he stopped to see what was left of the lion he had killed. He saw a swarm of bees and some honey in the lion. He took some of the honey in his hands and ate it. He gave some to his father and mother, and they ate some, too. They did not know that the honey had come from a dead lion. Samson did not tell them where he had gotten it.

# Samson's Riddle

Judges 14:10-18

Samson and his father and mother went on to where the woman was, and Samson married her. Samson made a great feast as the young men used to do at that time. Samson had thirty people with him at the feast.

Samson said to them, "I will ask you a riddle. If you can tell me the answer to this riddle in seven days, while we are feasting, I will give you thirty sets of clothing. But if you cannot tell me the answer, you must give me thirty sets of clothing."

To this the men seemed to agree, for they said, "Tell your riddle so that we may hear it."

This is the riddle Samson gave to

them: "Out of the eater came forth meat, and out of the strong came forth sweetness." They were to guess what the eater could be out of which could come something sweet. This riddle was about the lion in which Samson had found honey. A lion can eat, so it is an eater. Also, a lion is strong. And out of this lion Samson had taken sweet honey.

But the men did not know about this, and they could not guess the riddle. On the seventh day they came to Samson's wife and said, "Try to get your husband to tell you the answer to the riddle so that you can tell it to us, or we might burn you and your father's house with fire."

Samson's wife tried very hard to find out the answer to this riddle. She cried when she asked Samson to tell her the answer. She said, "You hate me. You gave a riddle to my people, and you do not tell me the answer."

But Samson said, "I did not tell even

my father and mother the answer to the riddle, so should I tell you the answer?"

Every day for seven days his wife came to Samson and cried, begging him to tell her the answer to the riddle. Finally, on the seventh day, the last day of the feast, he told her the answer to the riddle. Then she quickly went and told her people the answer Samson had told her.

So on the last day of the feast, the people told Samson the answer to the riddle. They said, "What is sweeter than honey, and what is stronger than a lion?"

Samson knew they had gotten the answer from his wife. He told them that if they would not have gotten the answer from her, they would not have been able to guess it.

## Lesson 27

# How Samson Treated the Philistines

Judges 14:19-15:8

Samson was angry because the men had found out from his wife the answer to to the riddle. Because he had promised to give them thirty sets of clothes, he did what he said. He killed thirty Philistine men and took their clothes off them. He gave the clothes to the men who had told him the answer to the riddle. Then Samson went home. He did not take his wife along because he was angry. Her father thought Samson did not like her anymore. He gave her to another man to be his wife.

After a while Samson went back to visit his wife. He took along a present to give to her. He wanted to see her, but her father would not let him. He told

Samson that he thought he hated her, so he had given her to be the wife of another man. But her father said, "Her younger sister is prettier than she is. You may have her."

Samson was not pleased that he could not have the wife he wanted. He said he was going to do to the Philistines something they would not like.

He caught three hundred foxes. He put them in groups of two and tied their tails together. He tied something in with the tails to make them burn. Then he set the tails on fire and let the foxes run into the fields of the Philistines. Of course, the foxes ran to try to get away from the fire. This spread the fire through the Philistines' crops and burned them.

When the Philistines saw what had happened, they asked, "Who did this?"

Some of the people answered, "Samson did it because his wife was taken away from him and given to another man." So the Philistines burned her father's house with fire. But Samson still was not satisfied. He killed many more of the Philistines.

# How God Helped Samson

Judges 15:9-16:3

The Philistines went out to the people of Israel as though they were going to fight with them. The men of Israel said, "Why do you come here against us?"

They answered, "We have come to tie Samson and to do to him as he did to us." The men of Israel did not know what Samson had done. So three thousand of their men went up to where Samson was and said, "Don't you know that the Philistines are ruling over us? What is it that you have done to them?"

Samson said, "I have done to them as they did to me."

The men said, "We have come to tie you so that we can give you to the Philistines."

Samson said, "Promise that you will not kill me."

They answered, "No, we will not kill you, but we will tie you and give you to them." They took two new ropes and tied Samson and took him to the Philistines. When the Philistines saw that they had brought Samson and that he was tied, they shouted.

But God helped Samson. The ropes became as weak as a plant that is burned with fire. They fell off his hands. Samson found a bone of an animal and killed a thousand men with it. Afterward he threw the bone away.

After this, Samson became very thirsty. He called to the Lord and said, "You have helped me very much. Shall I now die because of thirst, and shall these wicked people kill me?"

God made a hollow place in the bone Samson had used to kill the Philistines and had thrown away. Out of this hollow place came water. Samson drank this water and felt much better again.

After this Samson went down to one of the cities of the Philistines. Someone told the people that Samson was there. They watched all night at the gate of the city. They wanted to catch him when he left the city. They planned to kill him.

When Samson came at midnight he took the doors off the city gate and the two posts and walked away with them. He carried them to the top of a hill. God gave Samson strength to carry the gates away. So the Philistines did not get him after all.

## Lesson 29

# Samson and Delilah

Judges 16:4-17

After this Samson loved another woman. Her name was Delilah.

The Philistines could not figure out why Samson was so strong. They came to Delilah and said, "Try to get Samson to tell you why he is so strong and how we can get him. If you do this, we will give you a lot of money."

Delilah said to Samson, "Please tell me why you are so strong and what could be done to tie you."

Samson said, "If they will tie me with seven green twigs that were never dried, then I will be weak like another man."

So the Philistines came, probably while Samson was sleeping, and tied him with seven green twigs. Then Delilah said, "The Philistines are upon you, Samson." Samson broke the twigs very easily. They still did not know what made Samson so strong.

Delilah said to Samson, "You have made fun of me and told me lies. Please tell me how you can be tied.

Samson said, "If they tie me with new ropes that were never used, then I will be weak like another man."

Delilah took new ropes and tied Samson. Then she said to him, "The Philistines are upon you, Samson." Samson broke the ropes as though they were only a thread. The Philistines still did not know what made Samson so strong.

Again Delilah begged Samson to tell her why he was so strong and how he could be tied. Again Samson told her a lie. When the Philistines came to tie him, again Samson could just walk away from them. They still did not know why he was so strong.

Delilah said, "How can you say that you love me? You have made fun of me three times now and still you have not told me why you are so strong."

Day after day Delilah tried to get Samson to tell her why he was so strong. Finally he became so tired of it that he told her. He said, "There has never been a razor on my head. If my hair is cut, then my strength will go away from me, and I will be weak like any other man."

# A Sad End

Judges 16:18-31

Delilah felt sure that Samson had told her the truth this time. She sent for the great men of the Philistines. Perhaps they thought it was useless to come anymore. They had been fooled so often. Delilah said, "Come this once, because he has showed me the truth."

So the men came and brought money for Delilah. Delilah made Samson go to sleep. While he was sleeping, a man shaved off his hair. Then she said, "The Philistines are upon you, Samson."

Samson woke up and thought he could do as he had done before. He did not know that the Lord was not with him and would not help him. He was weak and the Philistines took him and put out his eyes.

They put him into prison and made him work. Poor Samson was blind and a prisoner of the Philistines. But Samson's hair began to grow again while he was in prison.

One day the Philistines gathered together to worship their idol. They said their god had given Samson to them. They praised their idol and had a good time. Finally they decided to have Samson come in so that they could laugh some more. They brought him out and put him where they could see him.

Because he was blind they had a boy with him to lead him. Samson asked the boy to help him get against the big pillars so that he could lean on them.

The house was full of men and women. Samson prayed to the Lord and said, "O Lord, please remember me and give me strength only once again so that I can pay back the Philistines for putting out my two eyes." Then Samson took hold of the two middle pillars that held up the house. He held on to the one pillar with his right hand and to the other pillar with his left hand. Samson said, "Let me die with the Philistines." Then he bowed himself with all his might and made the house fall down on him and on all the people. Samson killed more Philistines when he died than he did all the time that he was alive.

His brothers and others of his family came down and took him back home and buried him.

# List by Lesson

## Unit 1

### 1

breathed
Eden
fifth
fourth
green
nose
plants
rested
rib
second
seventh
shine
sixth
watered

### 2

coats
fruit
gods
hide
listened
longer
snake

### 3

Abel's

cries
driven
mark
punishment
raised
stand
tramp
wander

### 4

beast
broken
creeping
fountains
higher
pitch
resting
side
whole
wood

### 5

build
building
changed
flew
language

leaf
parts
thankful
waited

### 6

chose
cities
selfish
Sodom
Ur

### 7

hardly
married
warn

### 8

bound
brush
calling
feared
promises
prove
Sarah's

# Unit 2

## 1
becoming
bricks
dark-skinned
grandchildren
seventy
unhappy

## 2
among
flags
herself
hidden
Miriam
Moses
princess
thrown

## 3
drew
Egyptian
hitting
Jethro
lead
yesterday

## 4
holy
rod

sacrifice
shoes
tail
three-day
wonders

## 5
Aaron
deaf
father-in-law

## 6
drive
extra
lazy
Pharaoh
scolded
straw
themselves

## 7
burdens
magicians
stink
swallowed

## 8
either
frogs

jump
ovens
piles
serve
tomorrow

## 9
flies
lice
swarms

## 10
break
donkeys
handfuls
horses
sprinkle
stove

## 11
barley
flax
hail
lightning
mighty
mixed
spoiled
stop
thunder

thunderings

**12**

against
blow
bother
signs
stretch
thickly

**13**

borrow
firstborn
herds
midnight
neighbors
thick

**14**

fourteenth
important
lamb
posts
spend
tenth
yeast

**15**

dough
easily
million
missed
one-half
pillar

whenever

**16**

camping
captain
chariot
forward
lift
wall

**17**

fast
grumbled
healthy
palm
path
pull
sang
seashore
song
sweet
traveled
wheels

**18**

desert
manna
melted
quails
Sabbath
wafers

**19**

breakfast
overnight
stank
thirst
worms

**20**

gotten
heavy
held
hill
Hur
Joshua
win

**21**

edge
Mount Sinai
myself
shake
treasure
trumpet

**22**

commandments
countries
graven
image
lesson
rules
shalt
thee

thou
thy
vain

**23**

adultery
bear
commit
covet
false
honor
witness

**24**

beautiful
finger
tempted
write

**25**

calf
dancing

drank
fine
shaped
singing
soft
war

**26**

gate
Levi
shining
tribe
veil

**27**

grumbling
tabernacle
throughout

**28**

allowed
hasn't

**29**

beginning
brave
bunch
Caleb
carried
danger
enemies
faithful
giants
grasshoppers
leader
losing
overcome
pole
ripe
taller
weak

## Unit 3

**1**

closed
hole
screamed
screaming
wilderness

**2**

bloom
chosen
displeased
laid
nuts
remind

**3**

anger
bit
bitten
brass
hung

**4**

anyway
Balaam
curse
tonight

**5**

acting
crushed
flat
foot
further
imagine
narrow
ridden

**6**

disobeyed
nobody
valley
wear

**7**

Jericho
Jordan
Rahab
within

**8**

business
dried
rope

**9**

stepped

**10**

marched
shout

**11**

Achan
Ai
battle
chased
tore

**12**

chasing
hiding
running
spear
winning

**13**

cracked
Gibeon
join
journey
message
moldy
patched
split
tricky

**14**

cave
fought
Gibeonites
hailstones
settled

**15**

according
amount
certain
courage
Levites
refuge
remained
separate

**16**

deserve
table
thumbs
toes

**17**

dagger
Eglon
Ehud
eighteen
key
left-handed
locked
Moab
seat

secret
stuck
unlocked

## 18
army
Barak
hammer
iron
Jael
milk
nail
nine
pounded
thirsty

## 19
broth
cakes
dens
Gideon
job
meal
Midianites
nation
pour
staff
thrashing
wheat

## 20
Baal
bowl

dew
fleece
floor
grove
ox
satisfied
wet
wool

## 21
bun
counted
dog
knees
knock
lapped
lapping
twenty-two
won

## 22
Ephraim
fifteen
flesh
lamp
pitcher
scared
tear (tĕr)

## 23
Abimelech
Jephthah

## 24
flame
Philistines

## 25
bees
lion
roared
Samson

## 26
begging
clothing
eater
forth
riddle
sweetness

## 27
foxes
prettier
tied

## 28
afterward
hollow
ruling
strength
tie

## 29
Delilah
figure

razor
thread
twigs

**30**
fooled
lean
shaved
useless

# Alphabetical Order

## Unit 1

**a**
Abel's
age
almost

**b**
beast
birthright
blown
bound
bowing
breathed
bringing
broken
brush
build
building

**c**
calling
carry
catch
changed
chief
chose
cities
coats

creeping
cries

**d**
deer
dirt
discovered
draw
driven

**e**
eager
Eden
Egypt
emptied
empty
enemy
expected

**f**
famine
feared
fifth
finished
fix
fixed
flew

follow
fountains
fourth
fruit

**g**
giving
gods
good-bye
green

**h**
happens
hardly
harm
hide
higher
hip
hope
hunt

**i**
invited

**j**
jealous

317

**k**

kingdom
known

**l**

language
leaf
leaving
listened
loaded
longer

**m**

mark
married
marry
master's
minds

**n**

nearer
nicely
nose

**o**

older

**p**

parts

perhaps
pitch
plants
played
promises
prove
punishment
puzzled

**q**

quite

**r**

raised
rested
resting
rib
run

**s**

Sarah's
second
selfish
seventh
shine
side
Simeon
sixth
snake

Sodom
sounded
spread
stand
starting
stole

**t**

thankful
thoughts
torn
trade
tramp
trip

**u**

Ur

**w**

waited
wander
warn
watered
whole
whomever
woman's
wood

# Unit 2

**a**

Aaron
adultery
against
allowed
among

**b**

barley
bear
beautiful
becoming
beginning
blow
borrow
bother
brave
break
breakfast
bricks
bunch
burdens

**c**

Caleb
calf
camping
captain
carried

chariot
commandments
commit
countries
covet

**d**

dancing
danger
dark-skinned
deaf
desert
donkeys
dough
drank
drew
drive

**e**

easily
edge
Egyptian
either
enemies
extra

**f**

faithful
false

fast
father-in-law
fine
finger
firstborn
flags
flax
flies
forward
fourteenth
frogs

**g**

gate
giants
gotten
grandchildren
grasshoppers
graven
grumbled
grumbling

**h**

hail
handfuls
hasn't
healthy
heavy
held

319

herds
herself
hidden
hill
hitting
holy
honor
horses
Hur

**i**

image
important

**j**

Jethro
Joshua
jump

**l**

lamb
lazy
lead
leader
lesson
Levi
lice
lift
lightnings
losing

**m**

magicians

manna
melted
midnight
mighty
million
Miriam
missed
mixed
Moses
Mount Sinai
myself

**n**

neighbors

**o**

one-half
ovens
overcome
overnight

**p**

palm
path
Pharaoh
piles
pillar
pole
posts
princess
pull

**q**

quails

**r**

ripe
rod
rules

**s**

Sabbath
sacrifice
sang
scolded
seashore
serve
seventy
shake
shalt
shaped
shining
shoes
signs
singing
soft
song
spend
spoiled
sprinkle
stank
stink
stop
stove
straw

stretch
swallowed
swarms
sweet

**t**

tabernacle
tail
taller
tempted
tenth
thee
themselves
thick
thickly
thirst
thou
three-day

throughout
thrown
thunder
thunderings
thy
tomorrow
traveled
treasure
tribe
trumpet

**u**

unhappy

**v**

vain
veil

**w**

wafers
wall
war
weak
wheels
whenever
win
witness
wonders
worms
write

**y**

yeast
yesterday

# Unit 3

**a**

Abimelech
according
Achan
acting
afterward
Ai
amount
anger

anyway
army

**b**

Baal
Balaam
Barak
battle
bees

begging
bit
bitten
bloom
bowl
brass
broth
bun
business

321

**c**

cakes
cave
certain
chased
chasing
chosen
closed
clothing
counted
courage
cracked
crushed
curse

**d**

dagger
Delilah
dens
deserve
dew
disobeyed
displeased
dog
dried

**e**

eater
Eglon
Ehud
eighteen
Ephraim

**f**

fifteen
figure
flame
flat
fleece
flesh
floor
fooled
foot
forth
fought
foxes
further

**g**

Gibeon
Gibeonites
Gideon
grove

**h**

hailstones
hammer
hiding
hole
hollow
hung

**i**

imagine
iron

**i**

Jael
Jephthah
Jericho
job
join
Jordan
journey

**k**

key
knees
knock

**l**

laid
lamp
lapped
lapping
lean
left-handed
Levites
lion
locked

**m**

marched
meal
message
Midianites
milk
Moab
moldy

**n**

nail
narrow
nation
nine
nobody
nuts

**o**

ox

**p**

patched
Philistines
pitcher
pounded
pour
prettier

**r**

Rahab
razor
refuge
remained
remind
ridden
riddle
roared

rope
ruling
running

**s**

Samson
satisfied
scared
screamed
screaming
seat
secret
separate
settled
shaved
shout
spear
split
staff
stepped
strength
stuck
sweetness

**t**

table
tear (tĕr)
thirsty

thrashing
thread
thumbs
tie
tied
toes
tonight
tore
tricky
twenty-two
twigs

**u**

unlocked
useless

**v**

valley

**w**

wear
wet
wheat
wilderness
winning
within
won
wool